PLANT-BASED AIR FRYER COOKBOOK

PLANT-BASED AIR FRYER
COOKBOOK

75 Whole-Food Recipes for Healthy Vegan Favorites

JANET AND MADDIE DOCKERY

Photography by Iain Bagwell

ROCKRIDGE PRESS

For general information on our other products and services or to obtain technical support, please contact our Customer Care Department within the United States at (866) 744-2665, or outside the United States at (510) 253-0500.

Rockridge Press publishes its books in a variety of electronic and print formats. Some content that appears in print may not be available in electronic books, and vice versa.

TRADEMARKS: Rockridge Press and the Rockridge Press logo are trademarks or registered trademarks of Callisto Media Inc. and/or its affiliates, in the United States and other countries, and may not be used without written permission. All other trademarks are the property of their respective owners. Rockridge Press is not associated with any product or vendor mentioned in this book.

Interior and Cover Designer: Patricia Fabricant
Art Producer: Megan Baggott
Editor: Van Van Cleave
Production Editor: Emily Sheehan
Production Manager: Martin Worthington

Photography © 2021 Iain Bagwell, Food styling by Angie Cruce.
Author photo courtesy of Marc Dockery

ISBN: Print 978-1-64876-395-3
eBook 978-1-64876-396-0
R0

To Gramps, Granny, and YaYa,
thank you for teaching us.

STUFFED ROASTED SWEET POTATOES, PAGE 73

CONTENTS

ZUCCHINI LASAGNA ROLL-UPS, PAGE **79**

INTRODUCTION

HELLO, AND WELCOME TO OUR VEGAN KITCHEN! We're so glad you're here. My name is Maddie, and I created the YouTube channel Vegan as Fork with my mom, Janet. That's right, she's a cool mom. You can think of us like your very own vegan Gilmore Girls—we're a mother-daughter/best friends duo, and we love eating and making delicious food. We are so excited to share some of our favorite plant-based air fryer recipes with you!

Our family has a long tradition of expressing our love for one another through food. My grandfather was a trained baker and a cook on a large cargo ship. He began passing his culinary knowledge on to my mom at a very young age, as she helped him prepare extravagant family meals on the weekends. Janet is the youngest of four and would often find herself home alone after school while my grandparents were at work. She used this time to read all the cookbooks in the house from cover to cover, and she even started to experiment in the kitchen by herself. Janet now has more than 50 years of experience developing her own recipes!

We began our plant-based journey when I was in high school, as we slowly began phasing meat out of our diets for ethical reasons. In

2009, I decided it was time to stop eating meat completely after I bonded with some adorable farm animals at a petting zoo. I immediately texted my mom and told her we were both going vegetarian that day, and she wholeheartedly agreed. After doing more research on the horrors of the dairy and egg industries, Janet decided it was time to give veganism a try in 2014. I wasn't sure whether I'd be able to give up animal products like cheese, eggs, and milk chocolate. But with each delicious vegan dish my mom created, I realized I, too, could thrive on a plant-based diet.

It can be challenging when you're first transitioning to a plant-based diet to find a balance between healthy meals and meals that will satisfy you the way your old favorites did. Mock meats and cheeses are very realistic in taste and texture and can be very helpful in satisfying a craving, but they are often expensive and not very healthy. And let's be real, most people don't want to spend hours in the kitchen each day struggling with complicated recipes that require expensive ingredients to try to make plant-based foods taste more flavorful. Luckily, the air fryer can help with all of this!

I will be honest: When we first bought our air fryer years ago, we had only intended to use it to heat up processed frozen foods. We didn't realize that the air fryer is capable of so much more. With an air fryer, you can make tons of healthy and inexpensive plant-based meals in just a fraction of the time it would take to cook them in the oven. And as an added bonus, the food comes out as crispy and delicious as if you had deep-fried it but with minimal to no oil.

In this cookbook, we're going to show you the many health benefits of a plant-based diet and how to stick with it. With 75 delicious air fryer recipes, you will learn to re-create your favorite meals and discover some new ones, all of which use healthy, whole-food ingredients. We'll also show you tips and tricks to really master the use of your air fryer and easily bring your meals to the next level. Sound good? Let's get cooking!

SWEET AND SPICY SHISH KEBABS, PAGE 82

CHAPTER 1

THE PLANT-BASED DIET, EXPLAINED

It's time to demystify the plant-based diet. In this chapter, we'll break down what eating plant-based really means, why it's beneficial, and how to adopt and stick with this diet. Plus, we'll walk you through all of our pantry and refrigerator staples to help you get started.

WHAT DOES EATING PLANT-BASED MEAN?

Plant-based eating is a large umbrella that covers numerous different diets, but it typically refers to a diet consisting mostly of food derived from plant sources. Some iterations of plant-based eating, such as a flexitarian or pescatarian diet, still allow for the occasional consumption of meat or fish, respectively. The emphasis in these diets is to consume more plant-based than animal-based food. On the other hand, vegetarians choose not to eat any meat, fish, or poultry.

Veganism encompasses more than just diet, as vegans strive to reduce animal cruelty and exploitation in all aspects of their lives. For this reason, they do not eat animals or animal products, including dairy and eggs, and do not use products made from animals, such as leather.

Perhaps the healthiest of all is the whole-foods plant-based (WFPB) diet. WFPB makes plants the star of the show! The goal is to eat foods in their most natural form, keeping them as unprocessed as possible, and typically the WFPB diet does not allow for any salt, oil, or sugar (SOS).

The recipes in this cookbook will contain no animals or animal products and only unprocessed or minimally processed foods. In addition, most recipes will not include added salt or refined sugar. Using the air fryer will also allow us to cut down on the use of oil, and some recipes will be completely SOS-free. Eating plant-based doesn't have to mean bland, boring meals, though; thanks to the air fryer, you never have to choose between taste and health.

THE BENEFITS OF GOING PLANT-BASED

There are many reasons a person may decide to follow a plant-based diet, from ethical to environmental to health. No matter your reason, by adopting this diet, you will be contributing not just to the health of our planet but to your own health as well. Following are just some of the numerous health benefits of plant-based eating.

Weight loss. Following a plant-based diet can help you shed pounds and maintain a healthy weight. According to the Physicians Committee for Responsible Medicine, the fiber in plant-based foods will make you feel fuller while consuming fewer calories than you would with meat or animal products, which contain more fat.

Improved heart health. Heart disease is the leading cause of death in the United States. Dozens of studies compiled by the Mayo Clinic have shown that a plant-based diet can help lower cholesterol and blood pressure and thus reduce the risk of both cardiovascular disease and chronic heart disease.

Better gut health. Researchers have discovered that gut health can affect other functions of the body besides digestion, such as immunity and even mental health. The increased fiber of a plant-based diet can help promote the growth of healthy bacteria in your gut.

Reduced risk of cancer. Numerous studies have found fewer cases of cancer in people who follow a plant-based diet, compared to those who do not. However, it is unclear whether this is due to the elimination of meat from the diet or the addition of more plant sources of food.

Lower risk of diabetes. According to a study published in the journal *JAMA Internal Medicine*, following a predominantly plant-based diet could lower the risk of developing type 2 diabetes by 23 percent.

EATING ON A PLANT-BASED DIET

Now let's get down to the nuts and bolts of a healthy, well-balanced, plant-based diet. In this section, we'll break down the best foods to eat and the foods that are best to avoid.

LOVE THESE FOODS

The following foods are all fair game, so eat up!

Fruits. As if being packed with vitamins, nutrients, and fiber weren't enough, some fruits, such as berries, are high in antioxidants, which can boost your immune system and help protect your body from disease. And don't forget about avocados! They contain healthy fats and no cholesterol—the perfect combination for a healthy heart.

Vegetables. It's important to eat a wide variety of vegetables, from dark leafy greens such as spinach and kale, to colorful peppers and squash, to cruciferous veggies such as broccoli and cauliflower. The more color you have on your plate, the better! Veggies are high in fiber, nutrients, and water, which will help you feel fuller with fewer calories than other foods.

Beans and legumes. This category includes protein-packed heavy hitters like chickpeas, lentils, peanuts, and versatile soybeans, which can be used to make plant-based milk, tofu, and tempeh. Studies have shown that incorporating more beans and legumes into your diet can lower blood sugar, blood pressure, and the risk of diabetes and heart disease.

Nuts and seeds. These are another important source of protein on a plant-based diet. Nuts and seeds may be high in calories and fat, but these fats are mono- and polyunsaturated, which studies have shown can decrease the risk of cardiovascular disease. Easily add them into your diet through nut butters or nut milks, have a handful of almonds as a snack, or top your salad or cereal with some sunflower or pumpkin seeds.

Whole grains. Given the choice, always go for whole grains over refined grains. Whole grains still have all three parts of the grain (bran, endosperm, and germ) intact, making them more nutritiously beneficial for you. Oats, quinoa, farro, and brown rice are just some of the many whole-grain options that can be used as bases for delicious, healthy meals.

Tubers. Starch is not the enemy! Starchy tubers like potatoes and sweet potatoes can provide you with the carbohydrates your body needs to keep you going. Plus, these are complex carbohydrates, which take longer for the body to digest, resulting in you feeling fuller for longer.

LIMIT OR ELIMINATE THESE FOODS

SOS. In excess, salt, oil, and sugar can lead to a multitude of health problems, including heart disease and diabetes. It's okay to use these ingredients in moderation, but many people have reported that after going SOS-free, their taste buds readjusted and whole foods tasted more flavorful than ever before.

Refined flour. To put it simply, the refining process removes the most nutritious parts of grains. Because it contains simple carbohydrates, refined flour is digested much more quickly by the body and causes spikes in blood sugar. Studies have shown that eating an excess of refined flour can contribute to obesity and diabetes. However, it is safe to eat in moderation.

Transitioning to a healthy new diet can bring up a lot of questions. But don't worry—we're here to answer them!

How will my body react to eating more plant-based foods?

One of the first things you'll notice is more frequent bowel movements. You're going to be eating a lot more fiber than your body is probably used to, and since the body doesn't absorb fiber, it has to go somewhere. Goodbye, constipation!

Will I get enough protein on a plant-based diet?

There is a common misconception that you won't get enough protein unless you're eating meat every day, but that's simply not the case. While it may take a little more attention and planning, it is definitely possible to consume the recommended amount of protein from plant sources such as beans, nuts, and soy-based foods.

Do I need to take supplements?

At a minimum, it's a good idea for anyone following a plant-based diet to take vitamin B_{12}, which is only found in a small number of plant sources, including nutritional yeast, nori seaweed, tempeh, and fortified foods. Some may choose to also take calcium, iron, and vitamin D, but these are much easier to obtain from plant sources.

Are all plant-based foods healthy?

We wish—but no. A surprising amount of junk food is "accidentally vegan," but that's because it contains tons of chemicals and sugar in place of natural ingredients. Also keep in mind that many mock meats and cheeses are highly processed and can be high in sodium. Always be sure to check the ingredient labels and focus on incorporating more whole foods into your diet.

Will a plant-based diet give me more energy?

Many people have reported that they have more energy throughout the day after switching to a plant-based diet. When you don't eat meat, your digestive system doesn't have to work as hard, and that energy can be redirected elsewhere. The addition of nutrient-dense plant foods will also give you a boost.

Highly processed foods. Replacement foods like mock meats and cheeses can aid in the transition to a plant-based diet, but they are often high in sodium and saturated fats. Try to phase them out of your diet as you become more comfortable cooking with natural whole foods.

Eggs and dairy. This includes milk, cheese, and butter, which are all produced by animals. Definitely a no-go if you are eating plant-based for ethical reasons! Otherwise, try to keep these to a minimum or eliminate them completely from your diet, as there are many plant-based alternatives.

Fish and seafood. Fortunately, there are numerous imitation fish convenience foods and whole-food ingredients, like tofu and hearts of palm, that can replicate the taste and texture of fish and seafood with the right seasonings.

Meat and poultry. This is the number one category that must be eliminated for a plant-based diet. Studies have shown that switching to plant-based alternatives will improve your health, help the environment, and, of course, improve the lives of animals.

STOCKING YOUR PLANT-BASED KITCHEN

In this section, we'll walk you through the essential ingredients you'll need to make the recipes in this book and continue on your plant-based journey.

PANTRY

When you have these ingredients on hand, they can be combined to make countless delicious and nutritious meals.

Baking alternatives. We always keep pure maple syrup, cacao powder, and chickpea flour on hand. These are healthier alternatives to granulated sugar, cocoa powder, and refined flour, respectively. We also love to use monkfruit sweetener, coconut sugar, and dates—often called nature's candy—as alternative sweeteners.

Beans, dried and canned. These include chickpeas, white beans, black beans, pinto beans, and dark red kidney beans. We like using canned beans because they are so convenient, but try to buy no-salt-added brands. Plus, the liquid from a can of chickpeas, known as aquafaba, can be used as an egg replacement or to help brown your food. You'll find it used in some of the recipes in this book.

Cooking spray. Avocado or olive oil spray can be used to keep your food from sticking to your air fryer basket or pan. It can also be sprayed over your food to enhance the texture and taste of the food as it crisps up.

Flavorings. We love to use coconut aminos, liquid smoke, balsamic vinegar, and apple cider vinegar to add complexity to dishes with minimal salt. Additionally, apple cider vinegar is good for gut and heart health and can also be used to combat acid reflux and heartburn.

Nutritional yeast. Also known as nooch, this ingredient is rich in vitamin B_{12} and gives food a cheesy taste. It can be sprinkled over prepared meals as a seasoning or used as a main ingredient.

Nuts and nut butters. Look for healthy nut butters made from peanuts, almonds, or cashews with no added salt, oil, or sugar.

Rice. We like to keep basmati and jasmine rices on hand.

Salt-free spice blend. These blends can add a lot of flavor to your meals without any salt. We usually make our own spice blend (see page 106), but in a pinch, we recommend the Mrs. Dash brand.

Seeds. These include ground flaxseed, hemp seed hearts, pumpkin seeds, and tahini (sesame seed paste). All are excellent sources of healthy fats. We use them often in salad dressings and as an egg replacement for baking.

Spices. Our favorites include oregano, basil, chili powder, granulated garlic or garlic powder, and granulated onion or onion powder. These build flavor in marinades, dressings, stews, and other dishes.

Whole grains. These include whole-wheat pasta, quinoa, oats, farro, and brown rice. Quinoa and oats can also be ground into flour and used in place of refined wheat flour.

REFRIGERATOR AND FREEZER

It's a good idea to keep these refrigerated and frozen ingredients on hand at all times. This way, meal prep will be a breeze.

Fruits, fresh and frozen. We love blueberries, apples, bananas, avocados, and tomatoes, but get what you love.

Leafy greens. These include kale, lettuce, cabbage, broccoli, spinach, and Brussels sprouts.

Lemon and lime juices. These are especially helpful in enhancing the natural flavors in SOS-free dishes. For optimal flavor and health, we prefer to use freshly squeezed juices, but bottled juices that are 100-percent juice, not from concentrate, are the next best thing.

Nondairy yogurt, unsweetened plain. We mostly use coconut- and oat-based yogurts because of their thick texture, but almond- and soy-based yogurts will work, too. We can't emphasize this enough—make sure you get plain (not vanilla) yogurt to use in savory dishes. We primarily use yogurt for baking but occasionally also as a plant-based replacement for sour cream.

Plant-based milk, unsweetened plain. This can include milk made from almonds, cashews, coconut, soy, oats, or peas. It's absolutely essential to avoid the vanilla flavors in savory dishes, so be sure to get unsweetened plain.

Tofu and tempeh. Both are wonderful plant-based substitutes for meat. Tempeh is especially gut-healthy because it is fermented. Tofu is basically a blank slate flavor-wise and will soak up whatever spices and seasonings you use with it.

Tortillas. You can use both corn and flour versions; just be sure to look for whole-grain and/or low-oil options.

Vegetables, fresh and frozen. These can include bell peppers, onions, scallions, potatoes, mushrooms, carrots, cucumbers, asparagus, artichokes, eggplant, and whatever else you like.

QUICK TIPS FOR STARTING (AND STAYING ON) A PLANT-BASED DIET

Whether you're just beginning to explore a plant-based diet or you're already an old pro, here are some of our tips for easing into plant-based eating and sticking with it.

Start by re-creating your favorite comfort foods with plant-based ingredients. As mentioned previously, the goal is to limit mock meats and cheese. However, when starting out they can be convenient and comforting replacements. While they're not as healthy as whole foods, they are very similar in texture and taste to the foods they're replacing. This will help satisfy your cravings as you slowly start to incorporate more unprocessed whole foods into your diet.

Plan out your meals and consider prepping them a few days or a week in advance. Meal planning and advance prepping can save you lots of time and money and prevent you from buying a lot of ingredients you won't end up needing. We like to prepare double the amount of dinner every night so we can eat the leftovers for lunch the next day.

Be open with your family and friends about your dietary needs. Chances are most, if not all, of your loved ones will be more than willing to accommodate your plant-based diet. But you have to tell them about it first! For holiday parties and other gatherings, offer to bring a plant-based dish to guarantee you have something to enjoy while also introducing others to plant-based eating. You never know—they may decide to give it a try themselves.

Do a little research before you dine out. Vegetarian and vegan restaurants and meal options are popping up everywhere as plant-based eating becomes more popular. Still, it's always a good idea to check a restaurant's menu ahead of time when possible. Indian, Mexican, Thai, Japanese, and Middle Eastern restaurants are typically very plant-based–friendly, with easily adaptable dishes.

Be kind to yourself. It's not uncommon for people to put a ton of pressure on themselves when they start eating plant-based. But you don't have to go from eating meat one day to eating only plant-based whole foods the next. Listen to your body and make the best decisions for you.

JACKFRUIT TAQUITOS, PAGE 59

CHAPTER 2

GETTING TO KNOW YOUR AIR FRYER

Now it's time to explore the ins
and outs of the air fryer. We'll take
a look at the most popular makes
and models to help you find the
best appliance to fit your needs.
We'll also give you step-by-step
instructions and tips to help you use
your air fryer to make delicious and
healthy plant-based meals.

BEST OF TWO WORLDS: PLANT-BASED AND AIR-FRIED

Plant-based eating and air frying are like the Lady Gaga and Tony Bennett of the culinary world: At first glance you wouldn't expect them to work well together, but they're actually a match made in heaven. Cooking with an air fryer helps bring out the natural, rich flavors of food and gives it the crispy texture that you'd normally only be able to achieve with deep-frying. This method of cooking makes the transition to a plant-based diet easier than ever.

Even if you're already thriving on a plant-based diet, the air fryer will help you cut down on the prep, cooking, and cleanup time for your favorite staple meals with minimal preheating necessary and the ability to cook one-pot meals. Plus, the air fryer will open up a whole new world of surprising recipes, since you'll be able to fry, bake, roast, and grill all with one appliance. To get you started, the recipes in this book can be made almost entirely in the air fryer. Of course, we'll show you how to make the best French fries ever, but we'll also share tasty dishes that will keep you feeling satisfied all the way from breakfast through dessert.

WHAT IS AN AIR FRYER, AND HOW DOES IT WORK?

An air fryer is a versatile countertop kitchen appliance that can give food the same crispy texture and delicious taste as deep-frying with little to no oil necessary. It's essentially a mini convection oven. You'll notice when you open up your air fryer that the basket you put your food in has perforations on the bottom. Instead of frying the food in oil, a high-speed fan blows hot air, usually from a heating element at the top of the unit, around the food. The perforations in the basket allow the convection to take place, with the hot air continuously traveling around the food. This concentration of hot air on the surface of the food gives it the same crispy texture that deep-frying would without the oil.

But the air fryer can be used for more than just the fried effect. You can prepare a full day of meals just using your air fryer. Roasting, baking, grilling, and even stir-frying are all possible. The air fryer will also cook food faster than a convection oven. You won't have to waste as much time waiting for the oven, grill, or pan to heat up, and cooking times will be shorter because of the convection-style cooking and the small size of the unit. And post-meal cleanup will also be a snap, since you'll only need to clean one appliance.

MAKES, MODELS, AND SIZES

As air fryers have skyrocketed in popularity, more and more companies are producing their own models of all different shapes and sizes. With so many different choices, each with its own unique features, it can be intimidating to anyone new to (or even familiar with) air frying. In this section, we're going to take a closer look at the air fryer and help you decide which one will work best for you—or better understand how to get the most out of the one you already have.

DEBUNKING SOME MYTHS

Let's clear up some of the most common misunderstandings about air frying.

Air fryers only fry food.
False! The name is misleading. An air fryer doesn't technically fry the food at all; the cooking method is actually convection cooking–in which a fan rapidly circulates hot air around the food to cook it quickly and evenly. The air fryer can give your food the effect of frying but also of baking, grilling, roasting, and stir-frying.

Air fryers can only be used to prepare processed convenience foods.
False! While they are great at that, air fryers can also be used to make healthy, whole-food, plant-based meals from scratch. They are also great for reheating and crisping up leftovers, like French fries or pizza, that would get soggy in the microwave.

I can set and forget my air fryer like a slow cooker.
False! It's best to stay close when using your air fryer. Many recipes will require you to pause cooking at least once to either flip over your food or shake up the basket. This will ensure more even cooking.

The more expensive the air fryer, the better.
Not necessarily! Don't get distracted by all the extra bells and whistles or unnecessary accessories. Focus on what size you think you'll need and check customer reviews before purchasing anything.

COMMON MAKES AND MODELS

There are two main types of air fryers on the market today: basket air fryers, which look a bit like a tiny spaceship, and convection oven–style air fryers, which look like a toaster oven. Both types use the same convection method of cooking, but they have different features and their own pros and cons, which we'll explore as we discuss some of the most popular brands and models.

BASKET TYPE

In general, the design of basket air fryers makes it easy to shake up your food mid-cook, which will allow for more even cooking. However, you won't be able to check the doneness of your food without periodically pulling out the basket.

The Instant Vortex Air Fryer 4-in-1 (from the makers of the Instant Pot) is one of the top-selling basket air fryers. The large 6-quart basket can fit a full 2-pound bag of fries, which makes it a great choice for families.

Many air fryers will also come with preset options in addition to the usual air fry, bake, roast, and grill. The COSORI 3.7-Quart Air Fryer comes with 11 of these presets, including Frozen Foods, Vegetables, Desserts, and French Fries. You can still set the temperature and cooking time yourself, but the presets take out a lot of the guesswork.

CONVECTION TYPE

Most convection oven–style air fryers take up more counter space than basket air fryers, but they also tend to have more cooking functions. In addition to the traditional functions, the Ninja Foodi 8-in-1 Digital Air Fry Oven can air-broil and dehydrate food. Plus, because of the glass door, you'll be able to see your food as it's cooking. The fans in convection oven–style air fryers also tend to be quieter. But be prepared to pay a bit more than you would for a basket air fryer.

WHAT SIZE DO YOU NEED?

There is a wide range of sizes of air fryers on the market today. On the smaller end, the GoWISE USA Mini Air Fryer has a capacity of 1.7 quarts and cooks enough food to serve one or two people, which would be perfect for an apartment or college dorm. For a small family, you'll probably want a capacity of at least 4 to 6 quarts. For larger families or people who entertain a lot, you'll want to get an air fryer with a capacity above 6 quarts.

In general, convection oven–style air fryers tend to be larger than basket air fryers. The NuWave Bravo XL Air Fryer Oven has a whopping 30-quart capacity and can fit a 13-inch pizza inside.

OTHER FACTORS TO CONSIDER

To save space, you may want to consider combining your air fryer with another appliance. For example, Instant Pot now offers an air frying lid that can be used with a number of its pressure cookers. You could also get an air fryer with two baskets instead of one, which would allow you to simultaneously cook two different foods at two different temperatures. And many convection oven–style air fryers come with extra accessories like a rotating mesh basket, rotisserie skewers, and multilevel mesh trays. It's easy to get caught up in all the add-ons, so think about what cooking techniques and accessories you would actually use regularly.

KITCHEN TOOLS TO COMPLEMENT YOUR AIR FRYER

With your air fryer and just a few other kitchen tools, you'll be able to make all the recipes in this book and so many more.

- ▸ **Aluminum foil.** Foil is a helpful tool both for steaming and to shield food from browning too much.
- ▸ **Blender or food processor.** A small blender will do just fine for these recipes, but we recommend a high-speed blender if you're making your own flours.
- ▸ **Knives and cutting board.** One good chef's knife is all you need.
- ▸ **Mister/spray bottle.** We use this to lightly and evenly spray oil, coconut aminos, and lemon juice.
- ▸ **Mixing bowls and measuring spoons and cups.** You'll need a medium bowl for mixing and a larger bowl for salads.
- ▸ **Pans.** You'll need a metal or glass pan, a silicone cake pan, a ventilated mini pizza pan, and silicone cupcake molds. The largest pan that will fit in a 2-quart air fryer is 5 inches. Larger air fryers will be able to accommodate larger pans.
- ▸ **Scoops.** A scoop keeps foods like cookies and falafel a consistent size for even cooking. We recommend 2-tablespoon and ¼-cup scoops.
- ▸ **Silicone mat or kitchen parchment paper and rolling pin.** These will make prep work a lot easier.

▸ **Skewers.** Wood or metal skewers are great for shish kebabs and holding certain foods together during cooking. Make sure you get a length that will fit in your air fryer.

▸ **Tongs and spatula.** These are helpful to transport and flip hot food.

AIR FRYING STEP-BY-STEP

Now that you've picked out the right air fryer for you, let's go over the basics of how to use and take care of it so you'll be able to enjoy it for many meals to come. Even if you've used an air fryer before, it's good to get a quick refresher.

PREPPING YOUR AIR FRYER

The following steps are necessary to prep your air fryer before its first use.

1 **Before you do anything else, read the user manual that comes with your air fryer.** It may not be the most exciting reading material, but each air fryer is a little different, and the manual will have important safeguards and other useful information pertaining to your specific model.

2 **Remove all packaging materials from the air fryer and any of the removable pieces, like the basket and basket base and/or any racks and pans.** Wash these removable pieces with warm, soapy water. Many of these pieces are also dishwasher-safe, but check your user manual to be sure. When the pieces are dry, place them back in the air fryer.

3 **Find a safe spot to put your air fryer.** Choose a level and heat-resistant surface, as it is possible for an air fryer to melt or crack certain types of countertops. Placing a silicone mat or tempered glass counter-saver underneath your air fryer can often prevent this, but as always, check your user manual for specific instructions. Keep the unit at least several inches away from the wall and never use it on the stovetop. Finally, make sure the exhaust vent is not blocked.

4 **Run your air fryer without any food in it to burn off the protective coating from the factory.** Check your user manual for specific instructions, but if none are provided, we recommend running it at 400°F for at least 10 to 20 minutes. You will most likely notice a strong plastic or chemical smell, but that will dissipate.

START COOKING

To cook food in your air fryer, follow these steps.

1 **Preheat your air fryer.** This step isn't 100-percent necessary, but we highly recommend it, as preheating will cut down on cooking time and help cook your food more evenly. Air fryers heat up much more quickly than ovens, so this will only take a few minutes. If your air fryer doesn't have a preheat setting, set your temperature and add a few extra minutes to the cooking time.

2 **Cut food into similar-size pieces.** This ensures even cooking. If you want, lightly spray the food with the oil of your choice to bring out more flavor and crispiness.

3 **Place the food in the basket (and do not overfill it!).** Keep in mind that the air fryer uses convection airflow to crisp up food, so the more space between the food, the crispier it gets.

4 **Set the temperature and time.** If you choose not to preheat your air fryer, this is the time to start it up. Select the appropriate temperature and cooking time (it may take a little longer if you don't preheat) or one of your air fryer's preset options.

5 **Check on the food mid-cook.** If you're using a basket air fryer, just pull out the basket to see what your food looks like. But be careful because the inside will be very hot! This is also a great time to shake or flip your food.

6 **Remove your food and enjoy!** It's a good idea to use tongs or a spatula to take out your food instead of just dumping it into a bowl. This will keep you from eating any extra oil or gunk that has dripped to the bottom of the basket.

7 **Always unplug your air fryer when you're not using it.** This keeps everyone safe.

CLEANING AND CARE

Finally, use the following maintenance tips to keep your air fryer in its best shape.

1 **Clean the basket or tray after every use using warm water and soap.** Check your user manual to see whether these components are dishwasher-safe.

2 **Clean the basket base after every few uses or sooner if necessary.** If you have a buildup of oil in the base, pour it into a jar and let it solidify before throwing it away. Wash the base with warm water and soap.

3 **Clean the vent, exterior, and interior of your air fryer at least a few times a year, depending on how frequently you use it.** As always, make sure the air fryer is unplugged and completely cool; then wipe down the whole thing, including the inner walls and heating element, with a damp cloth.

OIL, COOKING SPRAY, AND OIL-FREE AIR FRYING

Cooking with oil is a hotly debated topic in the plant-based community. Personally, we feel that when it comes to oil, moderation is the way to go, so we use small amounts of it in many of our recipes. In general, the air fryer requires much less oil than other methods of cooking to make a delicious meal.

When choosing a cooking oil, you should consider a few different factors: health benefits, taste, and smoke point (the temperature at which it burns). For example, extra-virgin olive oil has a lower smoke point than regular olive oil and therefore should be reserved for salad dressings and lower-heat cooking. Regular olive, coconut, and avocado oils have higher smoke points and are better for high-heat cooking, such as frying and air frying. Look for oil sprays (not cooking sprays) that are 100 percent pure oil (with no additives or propellants, which can damage the air fryer basket's nonstick coating). You could also buy a mister and fill it with your preferred oil.

If you want to cook completely oil-free, most recipes can be adapted. There are many whole foods that can replace the oil in baking, such as applesauce, bananas, or nut butters. For stir-frying, water can be used in place of oil. When it comes to air frying, aquafaba can sometimes be used to help brown the food, but there are some recipes where the oil can just be omitted completely.

TOP TIPS AND TRICKS FOR
USING YOUR AIR FRYER

Here are some quick and easy tips to take your air frying to the next level.

Don't overfill the basket. It can be tempting to fill your air fryer basket all the way to the top, but don't do it. Your food won't cook evenly or reach its maximum crispiness. Leave some room for the hot air to circulate. The more surface area of the food that is exposed, the more evenly it will cook. If necessary, divide your food up into smaller cooking batches. Smaller batches will cook faster and crisp up more.

Shake the basket. It's important to shake the basket mid-cook for certain dishes, like French fries and vegetables. For more even cooking, you want to make sure every surface of the food is exposed to the heating element. Some recipes will ask you to shake up the food once, usually halfway through cooking, or possibly even every few minutes. If you're using a basket air fryer, all you have to do is pull the basket out of the unit and shake it back and forth to toss the food. If you're using a convection oven–style air fryer or cooking something larger, like slabs of tofu, use tongs or a spatula to flip the food over. Be careful—the food and air fryer will be hot!

Convert traditional recipes to the air fryer. The air fryer can take your traditional oven recipes to the next level. But keep in mind that because of the convection style of cooking, the temperature will likely need to be lower and the cooking time will be shorter. Depending on the recipe, you should set the temperature 10 to 25 degrees lower and decrease the cooking time by about 20 percent. It's always better to set the timer too short and add extra time than to overcook and burn your meal. Don't be afraid to pull out the basket and check on your food periodically.

Plan ahead for easier cleanup. If you're using a convection oven–style air fryer, make cleanup easier by placing some parchment paper or aluminum foil on the drip pan. Just make sure that you're not preventing the air from circulating in the air fryer. You can also buy perforated parchment paper that is specifically designed and cut to size to fit in the air fryer basket.

A little bit of oil goes a long way. Air frying requires significantly less oil to crisp up your food than deep-frying, but for most dishes, you're still going to want to use a little. We recommend giving most foods a light spritz. Not only will this help them crisp up, but it will also help bind any seasonings to the food. It would be a good idea to spray them again when you shake up the basket for more even crisping.

Let's take a look at some of the most common problems and safety concerns that may arise when using your air fryer.

Why is white smoke coming out of my air fryer?
This could happen for a number of reasons. If you're cooking food with a high water content, such as vegetables, this is probably just steam releasing from the food and is totally normal. However, white smoke could also be the result of built-up grease burning in the basket base. For a quick fix, you can add some water to the basket base, but you should give your air fryer a full cleaning after you're done cooking.

Why is black smoke coming out of my air fryer?
Using an oil with a low smoke point, like extra-virgin olive oil, can produce black smoke. These oils cannot handle the high temperatures of the air fryer and will start to smoke, making your food taste bitter or burnt. Black smoke could also mean that the fan has blown food and/or seasoning onto the heating element and it is burning. If you see black smoke, turn off your air fryer and wipe down the heating element after it has cooled.

Why isn't my food cooking evenly?
Uneven cooking is most often the result of overfilling your air fryer basket. Try cooking your food in smaller batches, and remember to shake the basket or flip your food at least once during the cooking process.

Why isn't my food browning?
Surprise, surprise! Overfilling your basket can also contribute to food not browning. If the air cannot circulate properly around the food, it will produce more of a steamed effect than a fried one. Spraying a little bit of oil or aquafaba on your food can also help with browning. We recommend lightly spraying your food with olive or avocado oil before you put it in the basket. For even more crispiness, spray your food again halfway through cooking, after you shake it up.

Why is my food sticking to the basket?
Although most air fryer baskets come with a nonstick coating, some coatings are better than others. If you're experiencing a lot of sticking, lightly spray your basket with oil before you put the food in, and remember: no sprays with additives and propellants!

Why is the breading coming off my food?

If the breading is sticking to the basket, you should lightly spray the basket with oil before adding the food. However, if the breading is not sticking to the food, you should lightly spray the food with oil before cooking. This will act as a binder for the breading and weigh it down so that it won't be blown into the heating element by the convection fan.

ABOUT THE RECIPES

We've created a collection of recipes that are a decadent celebration of plant-based eating but are healthy enough to eat every day, including many classic dishes with a plant-based twist. Be sure to read the entire recipe from start to finish before you start prepping your ingredients. To make things easy, each recipe will also include nutritional information and a banner giving the air fryer function and temperature.

LABELS

Keep an eye out for these recipe labels, which will highlight the special qualities of each dish.

- **30 minutes:** Recipes that take 30 minutes or less to make, including prep time
- **5 ingredients:** Recipes that require just five or fewer ingredients to make, not counting oil/cooking spray, salt, pepper, and water
- **Gluten-free:** Recipes that don't contain any gluten
- **WFPB:** Recipes that are SOS-free and are made using only whole foods

TIPS

We've also included at least one of these tips for each recipe to help make them as easy and delicious as possible while fitting your dietary needs.

- **SOS-Free:** A tip on how to remove the salt, oil, and/or sugar from a recipe
- **Substitute It:** Alternatives for some ingredients that are more accessible, will give the dish a different twist, or are allergen-free
- **Air Fryer Tip (or Preparation Tip):** A clarification on cooking instructions or information to adapt cooking methods for different air fryer models

Let's get cooking!

FRENCH TOAST, PAGE 25

CHAPTER 3

BREAKFASTS AND BRUNCHES

QUINOA QUICHE CUPS

30 MINUTES • 5 INGREDIENTS • GLUTEN-FREE

The base for this eggless quiche is quinoa, which is often referred to as a superfood because it is nutrient-dense and high in protein and fiber. This recipe works well with all different types of vegetables, such as bell peppers, onions, mushrooms, and spinach, so pick your favorites.

MAKES 6 quiche cups
PREP TIME: 5 minutes
COOK TIME: 20 minutes

1 (10-ounce) bag frozen mixed vegetables, thawed
¾ cup quinoa flour
¾ cup water
2 tablespoons freshly squeezed lemon juice
¼ cup nutritional yeast
¼ teaspoon granulated garlic
¼ teaspoon sea salt
Freshly ground black pepper

1 In a medium bowl, mix together the vegetables, quinoa flour, water, lemon juice, nutritional yeast, granulated garlic, salt, and pepper to taste until well combined.

2 Spoon the mixture into 6 cupcake molds, dividing it evenly.

3 Place the filled molds into the air fryer and bake at 340°F for 20 minutes, or until the tops are lightly browned and a toothpick inserted into the center of a muffin comes out clean. Let cool slightly before enjoying.

SOS-FREE: If desired, the sea salt can be omitted.

SUBSTITUTE IT: If you don't have quinoa flour, blend ½ cup of whole uncooked quinoa in a blender until it's a fine powder.

AIR FRYER TIP: We like to use silicone cupcake molds for easy cleanup, but a metal muffin pan with a light spritz of oil will work just fine.

PER SERVING (2 QUICHE CUPS): Calories: 239; Fat: 2g; Sodium: 401mg; Carbohydrates: 39g; Fiber: 8g; Sugar: 1g; Protein: 16g

FRENCH TOAST

30 MINUTES • 5 INGREDIENTS

You won't miss the eggs in this French toast! Customize this dish with your favorite type of bread, from white to wheat to cinnamon-raisin. Serve with maple syrup, your favorite fruit, and a sprinkle of cinnamon if you're feeling decadent.

MAKES 4 pieces
PREP TIME: 5 minutes
COOK TIME: 10 minutes

1 ripe banana, mashed
¼ cup protein powder
½ cup plant-based milk
2 tablespoons ground flaxseed
4 slices whole-grain bread
Nonstick cooking spray

1 In a shallow bowl, mix the banana, protein powder, plant-based milk, and flaxseed until well combined.

2 Dip both sides of each slice of bread into the mixture. Lightly spray your pan or air fryer basket with oil and place the slices on it in a single layer. Pour any remaining mixture evenly over the bread.

3 Place the pan in the air fryer and fry at 370°F for 10 minutes, or until golden brown and crispy. Be sure to flip the toast over halfway through. Enjoy warm.

SOS-FREE: To eliminate the sugar in this recipe, use a sugar-free protein powder or one that contains an artificial sweetener, such as stevia or monkfruit sweetener.

SUBSTITUTE IT: To make this recipe gluten-free, use a gluten-free bread. Be sure to check the ingredients first, as not all gluten-free breads are plant-based.

AIR FRYER TIP: If your air fryer basket is mesh, it's best to use a mini ventilated pizza pan. The mesh will not work well with wet foods like this French toast. If you don't have a ventilated pan, a regular flat pan or even a piece of aluminum foil or parchment paper would also work.

PER SERVING (2 PIECES): Calories: 365; Fat: 11g; Sodium: 388mg; Carbohydrates: 48g; Fiber: 9g; Sugar: 12g; Protein: 22g

BLUEBERRY-BANANA MUFFINS

30 MINUTES

Most muffin recipes are high in sugar, but these have a natural sweetness from the blueberries and banana. Wait until your batter is all mixed up and divided into the molds before you add the blueberries. This will keep the muffins from collapsing. In addition, let your muffins cool before enjoying, as they will continue to firm up a bit after they come out of the air fryer.

MAKES 6 muffins
PREP TIME: 5 minutes
COOK TIME: 16 minutes

1 ripe banana
½ cup unsweetened
   plant-based milk
1 teaspoon apple
   cider vinegar
1 teaspoon vanilla extract
2 tablespoons ground
   flaxseed
2 tablespoons
   coconut sugar
¾ cup all-purpose flour
1 teaspoon baking powder
½ teaspoon baking soda
¾ cup blueberries

1 In a medium bowl, mash the banana with a fork. Add the plant-based milk, apple cider vinegar, vanilla, flaxseed, and coconut sugar and mix until well combined. Set aside.

2 In a small bowl, whisk together the flour, baking powder, and baking soda. Add this mixture to the medium bowl and mix until just combined. (Over-mixing will make the muffins tough.)

3 Pour the batter into 6 cupcake molds, dividing it evenly. Then divide the blueberries evenly among the muffins and lightly press them into the batter so that they are at least partially submerged.

4 Place the molds in the air fryer and bake at 350°F for 16 minutes, or until the muffins are lightly browned and a toothpick inserted into the center of a muffin comes out clean. Let cool before enjoying.

SOS-FREE: Substitute granulated monkfruit sweetener for the coconut sugar to make this SOS-free. It can be found in most grocery stores in the baking section.

PER SERVING (2 MUFFINS): Calories: 248; Fat: 3g; Sodium: 229mg; Carbohydrates: 50g; Fiber: 4g; Sugar: 17g; Protein: 6g

APPLE PIE OAT BOWL

30 MINUTES • 5 INGREDIENTS • GLUTEN-FREE • WFPB

Bring a little dessert to your breakfast with this warm and satisfying oat bowl. Oats are naturally gluten-free, but some brands may be processed in the same facilities as gluten products, so if you have a gluten allergy, make sure your oats are certified gluten-free. Bring this dish to the next level with a sprinkle of hemp seeds and either a dollop of unsweetened nondairy yogurt or a drizzle of natural peanut butter.

SERVES 2
PREP TIME: 5 minutes
COOK TIME: 12 minutes

⅔ cup rolled oats
1 apple, cored and diced
4 dates, pitted and diced
½ teaspoon ground cinnamon
¾ cup unsweetened plant-based milk

1 In a heatproof cake pan or bowl, combine the oats, apple, dates, and cinnamon. Pour the plant-based milk over the top.

2 Place the pan in the air fryer and bake at 350°F for 6 minutes. Remove the pan and stir until well mixed. Bake for another 6 minutes, or until the apples are soft.

3 Stir again and let cool slightly before enjoying.

SUBSTITUTE IT: Feel free to use any fruit you'd like in place of the apple. Blueberries, pears, peaches, and strawberries all work wonderfully.

PER SERVING (½ OF THE RECIPE): Calories: 222; Fat: 3g; Sodium: 35mg; Carbohydrates: 44g; Fiber: 7g; Sugar: 19g; Protein: 7g

HASH BROWNS

30 MINUTES • 5 INGREDIENTS • GLUTEN-FREE • WFPB

These crispy hash browns deliver the delicious natural flavor of potatoes without all the salt and oil. To keep this recipe SOS-free, make sure your frozen potatoes are 100-percent pure without any additives. If you want to add a little extra flavor, spray each hash brown once with coconut aminos just after they come out of the air fryer.

MAKES 4 hash browns
PREP TIME: 5 minutes
COOK TIME: 12 minutes

3 cups frozen shredded potatoes, thawed
2 tablespoons nutritional yeast
1 teaspoon No-Salt Spice Blend (page 106)
1 tablespoon aquafaba

SUBSTITUTE IT: You could also make this recipe with 3 cups of freshly grated potato instead of frozen. If you're grating the potatoes ahead of time, soak them in cold water to keep them from turning brown. When you're ready to use them, simply drain and squeeze out all the excess water with a clean tea towel.

1 Cut 4 pieces of parchment paper, each about 12 inches long.

2 In a medium bowl, mix the potatoes, nutritional yeast, spice blend, and aquafaba until well combined. Divide the mixture into 4 equal portions.

3 Place 1 portion onto the middle of a piece of parchment paper. Fold the sides of the paper together and then the top and bottom to create a rectangle about 3 by 5 inches. Use the palm of your hand to press down on the hash brown to flatten and spread it.

4 Unwrap the parchment paper and use a spatula to carefully transfer the hash brown to the air fryer basket or rack. Repeat step 3 with the remaining portions.

5 Fry the hash browns at 400°F for 12 minutes, or until they are lightly browned and crispy. Be sure to flip the hash browns halfway through cooking. Enjoy warm.

AIR FRYER TIP: If you're okay with oil, lightly spray some on your air fryer basket before placing the hash browns in it to prevent sticking.

PER SERVING (1 HASH BROWN): Calories: 92; Fat: 0g; Sodium: 7mg; Carbohydrates: 20g; Fiber: 3g; Sugar: 1g; Protein: 3g

APPLE-CINNAMON BREAKFAST COOKIES

30 MINUTES • GLUTEN-FREE • WFPB

Cookies for breakfast? Yes please! These cookies are healthy enough for breakfast and delicious as a dessert. We recommend making a double batch because they are guaranteed to disappear quickly.

MAKES 15 cookies
PREP TIME: 5 minutes
COOK TIME: 9 minutes

1 medium apple
1 cup oat flour
2 tablespoons pure
   maple syrup
¼ cup natural peanut butter
⅓ cup raisins
½ teaspoon ground
   cinnamon

1 Using a grater or a julienne mandoline, carefully grate each side of the apple down to the core. Place the grated apple in a medium bowl along with the oat flour, maple syrup, peanut butter, raisins and cinnamon. Mix until well combined.

2 Scoop out 2-tablespoon balls of dough onto parchment paper. Wet your hand to avoid sticking and flatten each cookie.

3 Transfer the cookies from the parchment paper to the air fryer basket or rack and bake at 350°F for 9 minutes, or until the edges of the cookies start to brown. Enjoy warm.

SUBSTITUTE IT: If you're not a fan of raisins, chopped walnuts would be a nice substitute.

AIR FRYER TIP: Don't worry about leaving space between each cookie in the air fryer. These won't spread because they don't contain oil.

PER SERVING (5 COOKIES): Calories: 384; Fat: 14g; Sodium: 14mg; Carbohydrates: 58g; Fiber: 6g; Sugar: 26g; Protein: 11g

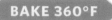

CINNAMON ROLLS

5 INGREDIENTS

You'll be amazed at how quickly these cinnamon rolls come together. Don't be fooled by the longer prep time, which is mostly just time for the dough to rise. We like to use a frozen pizza dough that is unbleached and unbromated and has very little oil. Feel free to use your own homemade pizza dough instead.

MAKES 8 rolls
PREP TIME: 10 minutes, plus 20 minutes to rise
COOK TIME: 8 minutes

½ (16-ounce) frozen pizza dough, thawed
⅓ cup Date Paste (page 112)
¼ cup natural peanut butter
½ teaspoon ground cinnamon
Nonstick cooking spray

1 On a sheet of parchment paper, roll out the pizza dough to about a 6-by-9-inch rectangle.

2 Spread the date paste and peanut butter evenly over the dough, covering it all the way to the edges. Then sprinkle the cinnamon evenly on top.

3 Starting from one of the longer sides, tightly roll the dough into a log. Using a sharp knife, cut the log into 8 equal pieces, being careful not to compress the dough too much.

4 Place the pieces, spiral-side up, in your air fryer basket or on a flat tray. Let the dough rest and rise for 20 minutes.

5 Lightly spray the rolls with cooking spray. Bake at 360°F for 8 minutes, or until lightly browned. Serve warm.

SUBSTITUTE IT: If you're allergic to peanuts or looking for a slightly different flavor, swap out the peanut butter for almond, cashew, or sunflower seed butter. You could also use whole-wheat pizza dough. Just give it an extra 10 minutes to rise.

PER SERVING (2 CINNAMON ROLLS): Calories: 270; Fat: 10g; Sodium: 298mg; Carbohydrates: 39g; Fiber: 3g; Sugar: 12g; Protein: 9g

TOFU SCRAMBLE BRUNCH BOWL

30 MINUTES • GLUTEN-FREE • WFPB

Tofu makes a great substitute for eggs in this dish! We find that medium-firm tofu is closest to the consistency of scrambled eggs. This dish is especially delicious when served with our No-Salt Hot Sauce (page 108) or No-Cheese Sauce (page 109) drizzled on top. And for a meal on the go, roll it up in a tortilla.

SERVES 2
PREP TIME: 10 minutes
COOK TIME: 15 minutes

1 medium russet potato, cut into fries or 1-inch cubes
1 bell pepper, seeded and cut into 1-inch strips
½ (14-ounce) block medium-firm tofu, drained and cubed
1 tablespoon nutritional yeast
½ teaspoon granulated garlic
½ teaspoon granulated onion
¼ teaspoon ground turmeric
1 tablespoon apple cider vinegar

1 Place the potato and pepper strips in the air fryer basket or on the rack and fry at 400°F for 10 minutes.

2 Meanwhile, in a small pan, place the tofu, nutritional yeast, granulated garlic, granulated onion, turmeric and apple cider vinegar and stir gently to combine.

3 Add the pan to the air fryer, on a rack above the potatoes and peppers. Continue to fry at 400°F for an additional 5 minutes, or until the potatoes are crispy and the tofu is heated through.

4 Remove the food from the air fryer and stir the tofu in the pan. Divide the potatoes and peppers evenly between 2 bowls. Then spoon half the tofu over each bowl. Serve warm.

SUBSTITUTE IT: If you don't like bell peppers, swap in other vegetables such as broccoli, onions, or mushrooms. One cup of thawed frozen vegetables would also work well.

AIR FRYER TIP: Lightly spray some oil on the potato and pepper strips before cooking for extra crispiness.

PER SERVING (½ OF THE RECIPE): Calories: 267; Fat: 6g; Sodium: 20mg; Carbohydrates: 42g; Fiber: 4g; Sugar: 2g; Protein: 15g

"SAUSAGE" PATTIES

30 MINUTES • GLUTEN-FREE

These "sausage" patties can really round out a breakfast or brunch. They have a nice smoky flavor that will remind you of actual sausage without the grease . . . or meat. Pair them with our French Toast (page 25) or Tofu Scramble Brunch Bowl (page 31) for a great start to the day.

MAKES 6 patties
PREP TIME: 10 minutes
COOK TIME: 12 minutes

½ cup oat flour
1½ teaspoons No-Salt Spice Blend (page 106)
½ teaspoon ground sage
1 teaspoon pure maple syrup
½ teaspoon liquid smoke
1 teaspoon balsamic vinegar
6 tablespoons boiling water
Nonstick cooking spray

1 In a medium bowl, combine the oat flour, spice blend, sage, maple syrup, liquid smoke, balsamic vinegar, and water.

2 Divide the mixture into 6 equal patties and place them on parchment paper. Wet your fingers and flatten the patties to ½ inch thick.

3 Lightly spray the patties with oil and place them in the air fryer basket or on the rack. Grill at 400°F for 12 minutes, or until the edges of the patties are crispy. Flip the patties over halfway through cooking. Enjoy warm.

SUBSTITUTE IT: In place of the balsamic vinegar, you can lightly spray coconut aminos on the patties after cooking to add a little more flavor.

AIR FRYER TIP: For easier cleanup and less sticking, use parchment paper in your air fryer basket. To keep the air flowing, use perforated paper or cut the paper into strips.

PER SERVING (2 PATTIES): Calories: 82; Fat: 2g; Sodium: 4mg; Carbohydrates: 13g; Fiber: 1g; Sugar: 2g; Protein: 3g

PB&J POWER TARTS

30 MINUTES • 5 INGREDIENTS • GLUTEN-FREE

These breakfast tarts will make you nostalgic for those childhood peanut butter and jelly sandwiches but are packed with enough protein to power a full-grown adult. If you don't like blueberries, feel free to use any type of fruit spread your heart desires.

MAKES 2 tarts
PREP TIME: 15 minutes
COOK TIME: 8 minutes

¼ cup natural peanut butter
1 tablespoon coconut sugar
2 tablespoons unsweetened coconut yogurt
½ cup oat flour
2 tablespoons Blueberry Fruit Spread (page 113)

SUBSTITUTE IT: It's totally cool to use a store-bought fruit spread in place of the homemade one. Look for sugar-free options or spreads that have been sweetened only with fruit juice. For a different flavor, ditch the fruit spread for our Date Paste (page 112).

1 Cut 2 pieces of parchment paper, each 8 inches long. On one of the pieces of parchment paper, measure out and draw a 5-by-12-inch rectangle.

2 In a medium bowl, combine the peanut butter, coconut sugar, and coconut yogurt. Once they are combined, mix in the oat flour to form a dough.

3 Place the dough on the blank piece of parchment paper and cover it with the other piece, with the rectangle facing you. Use a rolling pin to evenly roll out the dough to fit in the rectangle. Carefully peel off the top piece of parchment paper.

4 Using a sharp knife, cut the dough into 4 equal rectangles, each 3 by 5 inches. Place 1 tablespoon of the fruit spread on 2 of the rectangles and spread it out evenly. Carefully place the remaining 2 rectangles on top of the fruit spread and gently press on the edges with a fork to seal them.

5 Place the tarts in the air fryer basket or on the rack and bake at 350°F for 8 minutes. Enjoy warm.

SOS-FREE: Eliminate the sugar from this recipe by switching out the coconut sugar for granulated monkfruit sweetener.

PER SERVING (1 TART): Calories: 358; Fat: 19g; Sodium: 16mg; Carbohydrates: 38g; Fiber: 4g; Sugar: 14g; Protein: 12g

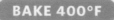

AVOCADO BAGELS

There's just something about a freshly baked bagel that starts a day off right. This one is super easy to make, with only three ingredients. (The rest are for the toppings.) If you don't like avocado, these homemade bagels would also be great with a tofu scramble or our "Sausage" Patties (page 32). And don't forget to drizzle some No-Cheese Sauce (page 109) on top.

MAKES 2 bagels
PREP TIME: 10 minutes, plus 15 minutes to rise
COOK TIME: 10 minutes

⅔ cup all-purpose flour, plus more as needed

½ teaspoon active dry yeast

⅓ cup unsweetened coconut yogurt

8 cherry or grape tomatoes

1 ripe avocado

1 tablespoon freshly squeezed lemon juice

2 tablespoons finely chopped red onion

Freshly ground black pepper

SUBSTITUTE IT: We like to use unbleached and unbromated flour, but these bagels can also be made with whole-wheat flour. If you're using whole-wheat flour, add another teaspoon of yogurt and double the rise time.

1 In a medium bowl, combine the flour, yeast, and coconut yogurt. Knead into a smooth dough. If the dough is too sticky, add more flour as necessary.

2 Divide the dough into 2 equal balls. Roll each ball into a 9-inch-long rope. Then form a ring with each rope and press the ends together to connect them, creating 2 bagels.

3 Fill a medium bowl with hot (but not boiling) water. Soak the bagels in the water for 1 minute. Then shake off the excess water and move them to the air fryer basket or rack to rise for 15 minutes.

4 Bake at 400°F for 5 minutes. Then flip the bagels over and add the tomatoes to the air fryer basket. Bake for an additional 5 minutes.

5 Meanwhile, cut the avocado in half and carefully remove the pit. Scoop the avocado out into a small bowl and mash it with a fork. Mix in the lemon juice and red onion.

6 Let the bagels cool slightly before cutting them in half. Divide the avocado mixture among the 4 bagel halves. Top each bagel half with 2 baked tomatoes and season with pepper.

PER SERVING (1 BAGEL): Calories: 375; Fat: 16g; Sodium: 27mg; Carbohydrates: 52g; Fiber: 9g; Sugar: 4g; Protein: 9g

SAMOSA ROLLS

30 MINUTES • GLUTEN-FREE

Samosas are traditionally made with a flaky pastry, but to cut down on the salt and oil, we've prepared these with low-sodium rice paper wrappers. And to change up the flavors, we've swapped out white potatoes for sweet potatoes. Yum!

MAKES 8 samosa rolls
PREP TIME: 15 minutes
COOK TIME: 15 minutes

⅔ cup frozen peas, thawed

4 scallions, both white and green parts, finely sliced

2 cups grated sweet potato

2 tablespoons freshly squeezed lemon juice

1 teaspoon ground ginger

1 teaspoon curry powder

¼ cup chickpea flour

1 tablespoon tahini

⅓ cup water

8 (6-inch) rice paper wrappers

1 In a medium bowl, combine the peas, scallions, sweet potato, lemon juice, ginger, curry powder, and chickpea flour. Set aside.

2 In a small bowl, mix the tahini and water until well combined. Pour the mixture onto a plate.

3 Dip both sides of a rice paper wrapper into the tahini mixture. When the wrapper starts to soften up, transfer it to another plate.

4 Spoon one-eighth of the filling (about ⅓ cup) onto the wrapper and wrap it up tightly, burrito style. Place the roll, seam-side down, in the air fryer basket or on the rack, and repeat this process with the remaining ingredients to form 7 more rolls.

5 Bake at 350°F for 15 minutes, or until the wrappers are lightly browned and crispy. Flip the rolls over halfway through cooking. Serve warm.

SUBSTITUTE IT: If you're not a fan of sweet potatoes, replace them with grated carrots, which also pair nicely with the ginger.

PER SERVING (2 SAMOSA ROLLS): Calories: 222; Fat: 6g; Sodium: 160mg; Carbohydrates: 43g; Fiber: 5g; Sugar: 5g; Protein: 3g

KALE CHIPS, PAGE **43**

SNACKS AND SIDES

AIR FRYER POPCORN

30 MINUTES • 5 INGREDIENTS • GLUTEN-FREE • WFPB

It's so fresh, quick, and easy to make oil-free popcorn in an air fryer. And the best part is you get to pick your own toppings. We like to fill a spray bottle with lemon juice and give the popcorn a light spritz first, which is essential to get the seasonings to stick without oil.

SERVES 2
PREP TIME: 5 minutes
COOK TIME: 7 minutes

¼ cup popcorn kernels
Lemon juice, in a spray
  bottle, for coating
1 teaspoon garlic powder
2 teaspoons nutri-
  tional yeast

1 Place the popcorn kernels in a single layer in a metal cake pan or in the air fryer basket, which should be lined on the bottom only with aluminum foil.

2 Grill at 400°F for 7 minutes or until the popcorn stops popping.

3 Transfer the popcorn to a large bowl and lightly mist it with lemon juice. Then sprinkle the garlic powder and nutritional yeast over the top. Toss to coat all the popcorn. Spray the popcorn again with the lemon juice and toss once more before enjoying.

SUBSTITUTE IT: For a different flavor, substitute our Mild Taco Seasoning (page 107) for the garlic powder and nutritional yeast. Or for sweet popcorn, swap out the lemon juice for water sweetened with stevia and sprinkle on some cacao powder.

AIR FRYER TIP: During cooking, keep the kernels as close to the heating element as possible. If you're using a convection oven–style air fryer, move the drip pan to the highest level and put the popcorn kernels on it. Then place the perforated rack upside down over it to create a popping cage.

PER SERVING (½ OF THE RECIPE): Calories: 119; Fat: 1g; Sodium: 8mg; Carbohydrates: 25g; Fiber: 4g; Sugar: 1g; Protein: 4g

CACAO TOASTED NUTS

30 MINUTES • 5 INGREDIENTS • GLUTEN-FREE • WFPB

This tasty recipe will work with a variety of different nuts, but cashews, almonds, and hazelnuts are our personal favorites. If you're making this with almonds, bake them for 1 additional minute.

MAKES 2 cups
PREP TIME: 5 minutes
COOK TIME: 4 minutes

2 cups raw cashews
2 teaspoons pure
   maple syrup
2 tablespoons
   cacao powder

1 Place the cashews in the air fryer basket or on the rack in a single layer. Bake at 350°F for 3 minutes. Then shake up the basket or stir the cashews. Bake for up to 1 additional minute, or until the cashews are lightly browned.

2 Transfer the hot nuts to a medium bowl. Drizzle the maple syrup over the cashews while tossing them to coat. Sprinkle the cacao powder over the cashews and continue to gently toss them until they're completely coated.

3 Transfer the cashews to a flat surface to cool. Store in an airtight container at room temperature for up to 2 weeks or in the refrigerator for up to 1 month.

SUBSTITUTE IT: If you don't have cacao powder, you can use unsweetened cocoa powder instead. We prefer cacao because it is less processed and contains more nutrients.

AIR FRYER TIP: Nuts cook quickly in the air fryer, so check on them frequently to make sure they don't burn.

PER SERVING (¼ CUP): Calories: 204; Fat: 15g; Sodium: 6mg; Carbohydrates: 13g; Fiber: 1g; Sugar: 3g; Protein: 7g

SOFT PRETZEL STICKS

30 MINUTES • 5 INGREDIENTS

These pretzel sticks will remind you of the kind you buy at the shopping mall without any of the oil and salt. We find the dough is easiest to work with if you let it sit at room temperature for 10 to 15 minutes before rolling it out. This snack pairs wonderfully with our No-Cheese Sauce (page 109).

MAKES 8 pretzel sticks
PREP TIME: 10 minutes, plus 10 minutes to rise
COOK TIME: 8 minutes

½ (16-ounce) frozen pizza dough, thawed
Flour, for dusting (optional)
1 teaspoon baking soda
1 cup hot water
2 tablespoons sesame seeds
Nonstick cooking spray

1 On a piece of parchment paper, roll out the pizza dough to about a 5-by-8-inch rectangle. If the dough is too sticky, sprinkle a little flour on the parchment paper. Using a sharp knife, cut the dough into 8 (5-inch-long) strips.

2 In a shallow bowl, dissolve the baking soda in the hot water. Dip each dough strip in the baking soda solution, covering it completely. Shake off the excess liquid and stretch each strip an additional inch or two; then place in the air fryer basket or on the rack.

3 Sprinkle the strips with the sesame seeds and let the dough rest and rise for 10 minutes.

4 Spray the strips lightly with oil and fry at 400°F for 8 minutes, or until they are evenly golden brown. Flip the strips over halfway through cooking. Enjoy warm.

SUBSTITUTE IT: You can use any topping you like (or none at all) in place of the sesame seeds. Poppy seeds, everything bagel seasoning, and cinnamon mixed with granulated monkfruit sweetener are delicious alternatives.

AIR FRYER TIP: To accommodate a smaller air fryer, you can make these pretzels any shape you want. Also, make sure the basket or rack is outside the air fryer when you sprinkle on the topping so that the excess won't burn.

PER SERVING (2 PRETZEL STICKS): Calories: 164; Fat: 312g; Sodium: 433mg; Carbohydrates: 27g; Fiber: 2g; Sugar: 3g; Protein: 6g

NOOCHO CHIPS

30 MINUTES • 5 INGREDIENTS • GLUTEN-FREE • WFPB

The nutritional yeast in this recipe gives these chips a subtle cheesy flavor—hence the name noocho chips. You won't be missing the salt when you're hit with a burst of flavor from the lime juice. We recommend using a fresh lime, if possible, for a brighter flavor, but bottled juice will work, too.

SERVES 4
PREP TIME: 5 minutes
COOK TIME: 15 minutes

2 tablespoons nutritional yeast
1 tablespoon Mild Taco Seasoning (page 107)
¼ cup lime juice
12 (6-inch) corn tortillas

1 In a small bowl, mix together the nutritional yeast and taco seasoning. Set aside.

2 Pour the lime juice onto a plate and dip both sides of a tortilla into the juice. Shake off the excess juice and place the tortilla on a clean plate. Sprinkle a little of the seasoning on top of the tortilla. Repeat with the remaining tortillas, stacking them on top of one another.

3 Using a sharp knife, cut all of the tortillas at once into quarters. Place the tortillas in the air fryer basket or on the rack in a single layer. Some overlap is okay, but you'll need to cook these in about 3 batches.

4 Bake at 360°F for 5 minutes, or until the chips are crispy but not burnt. Serve immediately.

SUBSTITUTE IT: For a different taste, swap out the corn tortillas for flour tortillas.

AIR FRYER TIP: Put your seasoning in a shaker bottle for more even distribution. We also want to emphasize again how important it is that you don't overcrowd the chips in the air fryer. Overcrowding will lead to some sad, soggy chips.

PER SERVING (12 CHIPS): Calories: 168; Fat: 2g; Sodium: 33mg; Carbohydrates: 33g; Fiber: 5g; Sugar: 1g; Protein: 5g

ONION RINGS

30 MINUTES

Onion rings are traditionally high in fat, but these beauties are made without any oil. Plus, you can make them gluten-free by using gluten-free bread crumbs. These golden rings pair perfectly with our No-Cheese Sauce (page 109) or Super Ranch Dressing (page 110).

SERVES 4
PREP TIME: 15 minutes
COOK TIME: 14 minutes

1 large sweet or
   Vidalia onion
½ cup chickpea flour
⅓ cup unsweetened plain
   plant-based milk
2 tablespoons freshly
   squeezed lemon juice
2 tablespoons No-Salt Hot
   Sauce (page 108)
1 teaspoon No-Salt Spice
   Blend (page 106)
⅔ cup panko bread crumbs

1 Cut off and discard the top ½ inch of the root end of the sweet onion. Continue cutting the onion into ½-inch-thick slices. Carefully separate the slices into individual rings and set aside.

2 In a medium bowl, mix together the chickpea flour, plant-based milk, lemon juice, hot sauce, and spice blend. Pour the bread crumbs into a separate bowl.

3 Dip each ring into the chickpea batter so that it's completely and evenly covered. Then dip the rings into the bread crumbs and place them in the air fryer basket or on the rack in a single layer.

4 Fry at 380°F for 14 minutes, or until the coating is browned and crispy. Be sure to flip your onion rings over halfway through cooking. Serve warm.

SUBSTITUTE IT: For a different flavor, swap out the No-Salt Spice Blend for our Mild Taco Seasoning (page 107) or your favorite spice blend.

PER SERVING (¼ OF THE RECIPE): Calories: 127; Fat: 2g; Sodium: 110mg; Carbohydrates: 23g; Fiber: 3g; Sugar: 6g; Protein: 5g

BAKE 350°F

KALE CHIPS

30 MINUTES • 5 INGREDIENTS • GLUTEN-FREE • WFPB

Any type of kale will make a delicious chip, but we prefer to use curly kale. This variety has lots of nooks and crannies, which will hold more of the seasoning and crisp up quickly in the air fryer.

SERVES 4
PREP TIME: 10 minutes
COOK TIME: 6 minutes

1 bunch kale, washed and patted dry
2 tablespoons freshly squeezed lemon juice
2 tablespoons nutritional yeast
½ teaspoon granulated garlic
½ teaspoon granulated onion

1 Remove the stems from the kale and place the leaves in a large bowl.

2 Pour the lemon juice over the kale. Use your hands to massage the leaves, squeezing and tossing them until completely covered. Sprinkle the nutritional yeast, granulated garlic, and granulated onion over the kale. Gently massage the kale again until the seasonings are evenly distributed.

3 Place a single layer of kale in the air fryer basket or on the rack, being careful not to overcrowd. Bake at 350°F for 3 minutes. Then shake up the basket or turn over the kale. Continue baking for another 1 to 3 minutes, or until the edges just start to brown.

4 Keep the kale in the basket outside the air fryer for several minutes so it can finish crisping up; then serve.

AIR FRYER TIP: Cooking times will vary depending on the thickness of your kale. Check on your kale every minute after the first 3 minutes because it can burn very quickly. If you have a rotating rotisserie basket for your air fryer, this would be a great time to use it. Your kale will cook evenly without needing to shake up the basket.

PER SERVING (¼ OF THE RECIPE): Calories: 17; Fat: 0g; Sodium: 9mg; Carbohydrates: 3g; Fiber: 1g; Sugar: 1g; Protein: 2g

FRENCH FRIES

30 MINUTES • 5 INGREDIENTS • GLUTEN-FREE • WFPB

This is the big one—French fries! We believe russet potatoes make the best fries because they are typically long, straight, and unblemished, which makes it easier to cut all your fries into roughly the same shape and size. We like to leave the skin on, but you don't have to. When it comes to the flavor, anything goes! Feel free to add your favorite seasonings or none at all.

SERVES 2
PREP TIME: 5 minutes
COOK TIME: 15 minutes

1 large russet potato
¼ cup freshly squeezed
   lemon juice
3 tablespoons
   nutritional yeast
1 tablespoon No-Salt Spice
   Blend (page 106)

1 Cut the potato lengthwise into ½-inch-thick fries.

2 Pour the lemon juice onto a plate. On a second plate, mix together the nutritional yeast and spice blend. Dip the fries, one at a time, into the lemon juice. Shake off the excess juice and dip the fries into the spice mixture to completely cover them on all sides. Once covered, place the fries in a single layer in the air fryer basket or on the rack.

3 Fry at 400°F for 15 minutes, or until the fries are crispy. Shake up the basket or turn the fries over halfway through cooking. Serve immediately.

SUBSTITUTE IT: For a different taste, substitute our Mild Taco Seasoning (page 107) for the No-Salt Spice Blend.

AIR FRYER TIP: Be sure not to overcrowd the air fryer basket or rack! Cook your fries in multiple batches for more even cooking. And for extra crispiness, lightly spray your fries with oil before and halfway through cooking.

PER SERVING (½ OF THE RECIPE): Calories: 172; Fat: 0g; Sodium: 15mg; Carbohydrates: 36g; Fiber: 3g; Sugar: 2g; Protein: 6g

STUFFED MUSHROOMS

30 MINUTES · GLUTEN-FREE · WFPB

This delicious dish works great as an appetizer or part of a larger meal. As a bonus, save your mushroom stems to use in a stir-fry or soup. If you're not a fan of mushrooms, the filling still tastes wonderful on its own. Just roll the spinach mixture up into little balls and follow the same baking instructions.

SERVES 4
PREP TIME: 15 minutes
COOK TIME: 12 minutes

1 (10-ounce) bag frozen spinach, thawed
3 scallions, both white and green parts, finely chopped
¼ cup finely chopped roasted red pepper
¼ cup chickpea flour
1 tablespoon nutritional yeast
1 teaspoon granulated garlic
1 tablespoon balsamic vinegar
12 whole portobello mushrooms, stemmed
½ lemon (optional)

1 Place the spinach in a medium bowl and press it against the sides to squeeze out most of the water. Discard the water.

2 Add the scallions, roasted red pepper, chickpea flour, nutritional yeast, granulated garlic, and balsamic vinegar to the bowl, and mix until well combined.

3 Spoon a heaping tablespoon of the mixture into each mushroom cap and gently press it down. The mixture should cover the whole top of the mushroom.

4 Place the mushrooms in the air fryer basket or on the rack and bake at 360°F for 12 minutes, or until the edges of the filling start to get crispy.

5 Squeeze some fresh lemon juice over the mushrooms (if using) and enjoy.

SUBSTITUTE IT: If you don't have balsamic vinegar, replace it with lemon juice and eliminate the optional squeeze of lemon juice at the end of the recipe.

PER SERVING (3 MUSHROOMS): Calories: 109; Fat: 2g; Sodium: 82mg; Carbohydrates: 18g; Fiber: 6g; Sugar: 0g; Protein: 10g

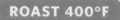

ROASTED ASPARAGUS

30 MINUTES • 5 INGREDIENTS • GLUTEN-FREE • WFPB

This lemony asparagus dish will bring you a little taste of spring any time of year. It's fancy enough for a get-together with friends and family but quick and easy enough to enjoy on a weeknight. We like to use pencil-thin asparagus, so keep in mind that thicker asparagus will need a minute or two longer to cook.

SERVES 4
PREP TIME: 10 minutes
COOK TIME: 5 minutes

1 tablespoon tahini
1 tablespoon freshly
 squeezed lemon juice
1 tablespoon water
1 teaspoon No-Salt Spice
 Blend (page 106)
1 pound fresh asparagus,
 woody ends trimmed

1 In a large bowl, mix together the tahini, lemon juice, water, and spice blend until well combined.

2 Add the asparagus to the bowl and toss to coat.

3 Place the coated spears in a single layer in the air fryer basket or on the rack and roast at 400°F for 5 minutes, or until the tips start to brown and the insides are cooked but not mushy. Serve warm.

AIR FRYER TIP: If desired, lightly spray the asparagus with oil before cooking. This won't so much affect the texture as it will enhance the lemony flavor. If you have a small air fryer, it's totally cool to cut the spears in half. Just be sure to keep them in a single layer.

PER SERVING (¼ OF THE RECIPE): Calories: 46; Fat: 2g; Sodium: 9mg; Carbohydrates: 5g; Fiber: 3g; Sugar: 2g; Protein: 3g

TWICE-BAKED POTATOES

5 INGREDIENTS • GLUTEN-FREE • WFPB

What's better than a baked potato? A twice-baked potato! This easy-cheesy dish will warm you up on a cold day and leave you feeling full and satisfied.

SERVES 4
PREP TIME: 15 minutes
COOK TIME: 35 minutes

2 medium russet potatoes, halved lengthwise
½ cup No-Cheese Sauce (page 109)
2 scallions, both white and green parts, finely chopped
1 tablespoon nutritional yeast

1 Place each potato, cut-side down, on a scrap of parchment paper in the air fryer basket or on the rack. Roast at 400°F for 30 minutes.

2 Carefully remove the potatoes from the air fryer. Scoop out the middle of each potato, leaving ¼ inch of flesh around the edges, and place the scooped parts in a medium bowl. Add the no-cheese sauce, scallions, and nutritional yeast to the bowl and mix until well combined.

3 Evenly spoon the mixture into the potato skins and place them back in the air fryer. Grill at 400° for 3 to 4 minutes, or until the tops get crispy. Serve warm.

SUBSTITUTE IT: For a sour cream and onion–style potato, swap out the No-Cheese Sauce for our Super Ranch Dressing (page 110).

AIR FRYER TIP: Don't cover the whole bottom of the air fryer basket or rack with parchment paper, as this will prevent the air from circulating. Use scraps of parchment just large enough to fit under each potato. This will allow the inside of the potato to steam while keeping the outside crispy.

PER SERVING (½ POTATO): Calories: 178; Fat: 21g; Sodium: 26mg; Carbohydrates: 37g; Fiber: 3g; Sugar: 1g; Protein: 7g

BABA GHANOUSH

GLUTEN-FREE • WFPB

This lemony and garlicky baba ghanoush is a great alternative to hummus, which typically contains a lot of oil. You can enjoy it as a dip for veggies or crackers or even use it as a light and creamy pasta sauce.

SERVES 2
PREP TIME: 10 minutes
COOK TIME: 30 minutes

1 medium eggplant
2 tablespoons tahini
2 tablespoons freshly
   squeezed lemon juice
1 teaspoon granulated garlic
¼ teaspoon ground cumin
Freshly chopped parsley,
   for garnish

1 Place the whole eggplant in a pan in the air fryer. Roast at 400°F for 30 minutes, carefully turning the eggplant over halfway through cooking.

2 Let the eggplant cool for 5 to 10 minutes. Then scoop out the flesh and place it in a medium bowl. Drain as much water from the eggplant flesh as possible.

3 Add the tahini, lemon juice, granulated garlic, and cumin to the bowl. Mix until well combined. Garnish with the parsley.

AIR FRYER TIP: We like to use a silicone cake pan because it cools off more quickly than a metal pan. If you don't have a pan, make one with aluminum foil so the eggplant won't leak all over the air fryer.

PER SERVING (½ OF THE RECIPE): Calories: 169; Fat: 9g; Sodium: 26mg; Carbohydrates: 22g; Fiber: 10g; Sugar: 10g; Protein: 6g

SPINACH AND ARTICHOKE DIP

30 MINUTES • GLUTEN-FREE • WFPB

We like to use frozen artichokes for this recipe to avoid the oil and salt typically found in jarred artichokes. If you do want to use jarred artichokes, look for the ones that are packed in water instead of oil, but keep in mind they'll still have a small amount of added salt. We recommend enjoying this creamy dip with our Noocho Chips (page 41) or some fresh veggies.

SERVES 3
PREP TIME: 10 minutes
COOK TIME: 20 minutes

½ (10-ounce) bag frozen spinach, thawed

½ (10-ounce) bag frozen artichokes, thawed and finely chopped

2 scallions, both white and green parts, finely chopped

½ cup raw cashews

½ cup unsweetened plain plant-based milk

3 tablespoons freshly squeezed lemon juice

1½ tablespoons nutritional yeast

2 teaspoons tapioca flour

1 teaspoon No-Salt Spice Blend (page 106)

1 Place the spinach, artichokes, and scallions in a pan and set aside.

2 In a blender, blend the cashews, plant-based milk, lemon juice, nutritional yeast, tapioca flour, and spice blend on high until smooth. Then pour the mixture over the spinach, artichokes, and scallions.

3 Place the pan in the air fryer and bake at 360°F for 20 minutes. Take the dip out every 5 minutes during cooking to stir. Serve warm.

SUBSTITUTE IT: If you're allergic to nuts or don't like cashews, swap out the cashews for hemp seed hearts or sunflower seeds. And if you don't have tapioca flour, all-purpose flour will work fine for this recipe.

AIR FRYER TIP: You can use any type of pan for this recipe, but silicone will be easier to clean.

PER SERVING (⅓ OF THE RECIPE): Calories: 208; Fat: 12g; Sodium: 111mg; Carbohydrates: 18g; Fiber: 6g; Sugar: 3g; Protein: 12g

CITRUS-ROASTED BRUSSELS SPROUTS

30 MINUTES • 5 INGREDIENTS • GLUTEN-FREE • WFPB

Brussels sprouts make a wonderful side dish for any meal, as they are low in calories and high in nutrients, including vitamins K and C. We typically cut our sprouts into quarters so that they'll soak up more of the orange juice, but if you're preparing smaller ones, you can just cut them in half.

SERVES 4
PREP TIME: 10 minutes
COOK TIME: 10 minutes

¼ cup freshly squeezed
   orange juice
1 teaspoon pure
   maple syrup
1 tablespoon
   balsamic vinegar
1 pound Brussels sprouts,
   trimmed and quartered

1 In a large bowl, whisk together the orange juice, maple syrup, and balsamic vinegar. Add the Brussels sprouts to the bowl and toss until well coated.

2 Place the Brussels sprouts, cut-side up, in a single layer in the air fryer basket or on the rack. Roast at 400°F for 10 minutes, or until they start to crisp up. Be careful not to burn them!

SUBSTITUTE IT: If you don't have maple syrup, substitute 1 teaspoon of coconut sugar or agave syrup.

AIR FRYER TIP: For extra crispiness and to seal in the orange flavor, lightly spray the Brussels sprouts with oil before cooking. Keep a close eye on the sprouts during the last few minutes of cooking. If the sugar in the maple syrup starts to burn, it will make the sprouts taste bitter.

PER SERVING (¼ OF THE RECIPE): Calories: 64; Fat: 0g; Sodium: 30mg; Carbohydrates: 14g; Fiber: 4g; Sugar: 5g; Protein: 4g

EASY FALAFEL SALAD, PAGE 57

CHAPTER 5

SALADS AND HANDHELDS

GRILLED ROMAINE SALAD

30 MINUTES

We know it sounds weird to put lettuce in an air fryer, but trust us, you won't regret it! This stunning salad not only looks beautiful, but it also delivers in the flavor department. The grilled veggies are already delicious on their own, but the dressing and croutons really pull the whole dish together.

SERVES 4
PREP TIME: 10 minutes
COOK TIME: 16 minutes

2 tablespoons Almond Ricotta (page 115)

1 teaspoon granulated garlic

2 slices whole-grain bread

1 cup frozen corn kernels, thawed

1 pound asparagus, woody ends trimmed

2 medium heads romaine lettuce, halved lengthwise

16 cherry or grape tomatoes, halved

¼ cup thinly sliced red onion

½ cup Super Ranch Dressing (page 110)

SUBSTITUTE IT: You can use any type of bread you'd like to make the croutons. Using Ezekiel bread would make this WFPB, and you can use gluten-free bread to make this dish gluten-free.

1 In a small bowl, mix together the almond ricotta and granulated garlic. Spread half of the mixture onto one side of each slice of bread. Place the bread in the air fryer basket or on the rack, spread-side up, and grill at 400°F for 2 minutes, or until toasted. Let the bread cool slightly before cutting it into croutons. Set aside.

2 Place the corn in a pan in the air fryer. Grill at 400°F for 4 minutes. Set aside.

3 Cut each asparagus spear into 3 pieces. Place the asparagus in a single layer in the air fryer basket or on the rack and grill at 400°F for 7 minutes, or until the asparagus are crisp-tender. Set aside.

4 Place the romaine halves in the air fryer, cut-side up, and grill at 400°F for 3 minutes, or until the leaves start to wilt and brown.

5 Remove the romaine halves from the air fryer and place each on its own plate. Equally divide the croutons, corn, asparagus, tomatoes, and red onion among each salad. Drizzle 2 tablespoons ranch dressing over each salad. Serve immediately.

AIR FRYER TIP: We usually like to use pencil-thin asparagus, but if you're using thicker ones, add 1 to 2 additional minutes to the cook time.

PER SERVING (¼ OF THE RECIPE): Calories: 212; Fat: 3g; Sodium: 109mg; Carbohydrates: 37g; Fiber: 13g; Sugar: 10g; Protein: 12g

ROASTED VEGGIE SALAD

GLUTEN-FREE • WFPB

This salad is a warm, hearty meal that will really fill you up. The magic of this dish is all in the layers. As it cooks, the juices from the mushrooms and tomatoes drip down onto the green beans and steam them, while the potatoes are roasting on the top. This eliminates the need to cook all of these delicious veggies separately.

SERVES 4
PREP TIME: 10 minutes
COOK TIME: 25 minutes

1½ cups quartered mushrooms
1 cup cherry or grape tomatoes
1 medium red onion, thinly sliced
1 tablespoon No-Salt Spice Blend (page 106)
1 (10-ounce) bag frozen green beans, thawed
2 cups fingerling or creamer potatoes
½ pound baby spinach
½ cup Lemon-Tahini Dressing (page 111)
¼ cup unsalted pepitas

1 In a medium bowl, toss the mushrooms, tomatoes, and red onion with the spice blend. Set aside.

2 Place the green beans in a large baking pan and cover them with the veggie mixture. Do not mix. Then place the potatoes on top in a single layer. (It's okay if the potatoes are above the rim of the pan.)

3 Place the pan in the air fryer and roast at 380°F for 25 minutes, or until the potatoes are fork-tender.

4 Let cool slightly before transferring everything to a large bowl. Toss to mix. Then add the baby spinach and toss again.

5 Drizzle the lemon-tahini dressing over the salad and sprinkle the pepitas on top. Toss once more and serve immediately.

SUBSTITUTE IT: Pepitas are shelled pumpkin seeds. If you don't have any pepitas, sunflower seeds would also add a nice bit of crunch to this salad. For a different flavor, swap out the Lemon-Tahini Dressing for our Super Ranch Dressing (page 110).

AIR FRYER TIP: If you have a small air fryer, divide the recipe into 2 smaller pans. We recommend using a metal pan for this recipe. Silicone won't get hot enough to cook the green beans completely.

PER SERVING (¼ OF THE RECIPE): Calories: 220; Fat: 8g; Sodium: 69mg; Carbohydrates: 30g; Fiber: 7g; Sugar: 7g; Protein: 9g

BUFFALO-RANCH CHICKPEA SALAD

30 MINUTES • GLUTEN-FREE • WFPB

This light, refreshing salad gets a zesty kick from the buffalo chickpeas. We prefer the taste of romaine lettuce, but this salad would also be delicious with iceberg or butter lettuce. As for the cucumber, peel it or don't, depending on how you like it.

SERVES 2
PREP TIME: 10 minutes
COOK TIME: 9 minutes

3 tablespoons No-Salt Hot Sauce (page 108)

1 teaspoon granulated garlic

1 (15.5-ounce) can chickpeas, drained, rinsed, and patted dry

12 cherry or grape tomatoes

6 cups chopped romaine lettuce

1 medium cucumber, thinly sliced

2 celery stalks, finely chopped

2 scallions, both white and green parts, thinly sliced

¼ cup Super Ranch Dressing (page 110)

1 In a medium bowl, mix the hot sauce and granulated garlic together until well combined. Then add the chickpeas and toss to coat.

2 Place the chickpeas and the tomatoes in the air fryer basket or on the rack in a single layer. Bake at 360°F for 9 minutes, or until the tomatoes are blistered.

3 Meanwhile, assemble the rest of the salad. In a large bowl, toss together the romaine lettuce, cucumber, celery, and scallions. Pour the ranch dressing on top and toss again.

4 Remove the chickpeas and tomatoes from the air fryer and add them to the salad. Serve immediately.

SUBSTITUTE IT: Feel free to swap out the No-Salt Hot Sauce for your favorite homemade or store-bought hot sauce.

PER SERVING (½ OF THE RECIPE): Calories: 301; Fat: 5g; Sodium: 65mg; Carbohydrates: 49g; Fiber: 16g; Sugar: 13g; Protein: 17g

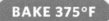
EASY FALAFEL SALAD

30 MINUTES • GLUTEN-FREE • WFPB

Falafel is traditionally made with dried chickpeas that have been soaked overnight and then ground to make the patties. We've shortened the process without sacrificing any of the flavor by using canned chickpeas and chickpea flour. This is one of our favorite go-to salads since going vegan.

SERVES 2
PREP TIME: 15 minutes
COOK TIME: 12 minutes

1 (15.5-ounce) can chick-
   peas, drained and rinsed
½ cup thinly sliced red
   onion, divided
⅓ cup finely chopped fresh
   cilantro
2 tablespoons freshly
   squeezed lemon juice
1 teaspoon granulated garlic
1 teaspoon ground cumin
¼ cup chickpea flour
6 cups chopped
   romaine lettuce
1 cup cherry or grape
   tomatoes, halved
1 medium cucumber, peeled
   and cut into rounds
¼ cup Lemon-Tahini
   Dressing (page 111)

1 In a medium bowl, use a fork to roughly mash the chickpeas. Add ¼ cup red onion, the cilantro, lemon juice, granulated garlic, cumin, and chickpea flour and mix until well combined.

2 Use your hands to shape the mixture into 8 equal patties.

3 Place the patties in the air fryer basket or on the rack in a single layer and bake at 375°F for 12 minutes, or until they are lightly browned. Flip the patties over halfway through cooking.

4 Meanwhile, assemble the rest of the salad. In a large bowl, toss together the romaine lettuce, tomatoes, cucumber, and remaining ¼ cup red onion.

5 Let the falafel cool slightly before adding it to the salad. Pour the lemon-tahini dressing over the top and give the salad a final toss before serving.

SUBSTITUTE IT: If you don't have chickpea flour, you can substitute all-purpose flour, but then the salad won't be gluten-free. If you prefer fresh garlic, use 2 minced cloves instead of the granulated garlic. Finally, if you aren't a fan of cilantro, swap it out for fresh parsley.

AIR FRYER TIP: If desired, lightly spray the falafel with oil before cooking for extra crispiness.

PER SERVING (½ OF THE RECIPE): Calories: 386; Fat: 9g; Sodium: 47mg; Carbohydrates: 59g; Fiber: 17g; Sugar: 16g; Protein: 18g

CRABLESS CAKES

30 MINUTES ▪ GLUTEN-FREE

The appetizing smell of these "crab" cakes will transport you to the seaside. Dulse granules, made from seaweed, bring in the flavor of the ocean. We've replaced the traditional cracker crumbs with chickpea flour for a healthier option that packs a punch of protein. Take it to the next level and serve with vegan tartar sauce or coleslaw.

MAKES 6 patties
PREP TIME: 10 minutes
COOK TIME: 15 minutes

1 (14-ounce) can whole
    hearts of palm, drained
    and rinsed
½ green or red bell
    pepper, seeded and
    finely chopped
3 scallions, both white
    and green parts,
    finely chopped
¼ teaspoon
    granulated garlic
1 teaspoon dulse granules
2 tablespoons freshly
    squeezed lemon juice
2 tablespoons vegan
    mayonnaise
1 cup chickpea flour

1   Run a fork lengthwise along each heart of palm to shred it. Place the shreds in a medium bowl along with the bell pepper, scallions, granulated garlic, dulse granules, lemon juice, and vegan mayonnaise. Mix until well combined. Then add the chickpea flour and mix until all of the flour is incorporated.

2   Wet your hands to prevent sticking and form the mixture into 6 equal patties.

3   Place the patties in the air fryer basket or on the rack, leaving a little space in between them. Fry at 400°F for 15 minutes, or until browned and crispy. Be sure to flip the cakes halfway through. Enjoy warm.

SUBSTITUTE IT: If you don't have hearts of palm, artichoke hearts or jackfruit will sub in just fine. And if you don't have dulse granules, finely chop ½ sheet of nori instead.

AIR FRYER TIP: If you're okay with oil, lightly spray some on your air fryer basket or rack before placing the crabless cakes in it to prevent sticking.

PER SERVING (2 PATTIES): Calories: 192; Fat: 6g; Sodium: 243mg; Carbohydrates: 26g; Fiber: 7g; Sugar: 5g; Protein: 11g

JACKFRUIT TAQUITOS

GLUTEN-FREE • WFPB

The stringy texture of jackfruit makes it a great replacement for meat. But be sure to use young green jackfruit and not ripe jackfruit, which has a sweet flavor. To enjoy these taquitos to the fullest, drizzle some No-Cheese Sauce (page 109) over the top and dig in.

MAKES 12 taquitos
PREP TIME: 15 minutes
COOK TIME: 20 minutes

1 (15.5-ounce) can dark red kidney beans, drained and rinsed

1 (20-ounce) can young green jackfruit, drained and rinsed

2 tablespoons Mild Taco Seasoning (page 107)

1 tablespoon No-Salt Hot Sauce (page 108)

¼ cup finely chopped red onion

½ cup diced tomato

¼ cup finely chopped fresh cilantro

¼ cup freshly squeezed lime juice

12 (5- or 6-inch) corn tortillas

1 In a medium bowl, use a fork to mash the kidney beans. Then use your hands to shred the jackfruit and add it to the bowl.

2 Add the taco seasoning, hot sauce, red onion, tomato, cilantro, and lime juice to the bowl and mix until well combined.

3 Place a tortilla on a plate. Spoon 2 heaping tablespoons of the mixture onto the tortilla, keeping the filling close to one side. Roll up the tortilla, starting on the side with the filling. Repeat with the remaining tortillas.

4 Place the taquitos in the air fryer basket or on the rack, seam-side down. Bake them at 360°F for 20 minutes, or until the outside is crispy. Serve warm.

SUBSTITUTE IT: To cut down on prep, swap out the red onion and tomato for ½ cup of low-sodium salsa. You can also use your favorite hot sauce in place of our No-Salt Hot Sauce.

AIR FRYER TIP: To prevent the tortillas from breaking while rolling the taquitos, wrap them in aluminum foil and warm them up in the air fryer at 300°F for 10 minutes as you prep your taquito filling.

PER SERVING (3 TAQUITOS): Calories: 431; Fat: 3g; Sodium: 115mg; Carbohydrates: 91g; Fiber: 14g; Sugar: 24g; Protein: 16g

SWEET AND SPICY CAULIFLOWER WINGS

30 MINUTES • GLUTEN-FREE • WFPB

These tangy cauliflower wings bring the sweet and spicy flavor without any added sugar, oil, or salt. You can use frozen cauliflower florets for this recipe, but we like to divide a head of cauliflower between this dish and our Spicy Pineapple-Cauliflower Stir-Fry (page 70). When preparing your cauliflower, use most of the florets for this recipe and save the stems and core for the cauliflower stir-fry.

SERVES 4
PREP TIME: 15 minutes
COOK TIME: 15 minutes

¾ cup chickpea flour

2 teaspoons No-Salt Spice Blend (page 106)

3 tablespoons No-Salt Hot Sauce (page 108), divided

2 tablespoons freshly squeezed lime juice, divided

½ cup unsweetened plain plant-based milk

½ head cauliflower, cut into florets

1 tablespoon pure maple syrup

SUBSTITUTE IT: For a different flavor, swap out this sweet and spicy sauce for our Super Ranch Dressing (page 110) or our No-Cheese Sauce (page 109).

1 In a large bowl, whisk together the chickpea flour, spice blend, 2 tablespoons hot sauce, 1 tablespoon lime juice, and the plant-based milk. Add the cauliflower to the bowl and use a spatula to toss and coat the cauliflower completely in the batter. Scrape down the sides of the bowl when necessary.

2 Place the coated cauliflower in a single layer in the air fryer basket or on the rack. Bake at 360°F for 15 minutes, or until the coating is lightly browned and crispy. Shake up the basket or turn the cauliflower over halfway through cooking.

3 Meanwhile, in a small bowl, mix together the remaining 1 tablespoon hot sauce, the remaining 1 tablespoon lime juice, and the maple syrup until well combined.

4 After the cauliflower is done cooking, while it's still hot, either drizzle the sauce over it or use the sauce as a dip.

AIR FRYER TIP: Cut all of your florets relatively the same size for more even cooking.

PER SERVING (¼ OF THE RECIPE): Calories: 110; Fat: 2g; Sodium: 44mg; Carbohydrates: 18g; Fiber: 4g; Sugar: 7g; Protein: 6g

GRILLED DOUBLE "CHEESE"

30 MINUTES • 5 INGREDIENTS

This gourmet grilled "cheese" sandwich doesn't actually have any dairy at all. Instead of spreading butter or mayonnaise on the bread, we've used some of our No-Cheese Sauce. And in the middle, you'll find an ooey-gooey, creamy cashew mozzarella. Yum! Plus, you can make this with gluten-free bread or use Ezekiel bread to make this WFPB.

MAKES 2 sandwiches
PREP TIME: 5 minutes
COOK TIME: 7 minutes

¼ cup No-Cheese Sauce (page 109), divided
4 slices whole-grain bread
¼ cup Cashew Mozzarella (page 114)
¼ cup thinly sliced roasted red peppers
3 tablespoons thinly sliced red onion

1 Spread a light coating of the no-cheese sauce on one side of each of 2 slices of bread and place them, cheese-side down, in the air fryer basket or on the rack. Spoon half of the cashew mozzarella on top of each of these slices and spread it around. Then divide the roasted red peppers and red onion between each sandwich.

2 Thinly spread the remaining no-cheese sauce on both sides of the remaining 2 slices of bread and place 1 slice on top of each sandwich.

3 Grill at 400°F for 4 minutes. Use a spatula to flip over the sandwiches and grill for an additional 3 minutes, or until the bread is well toasted. Serve immediately.

SUBSTITUTE IT: For a different flavor, swap out the roasted red peppers and red onion for baby spinach and thinly sliced tomatoes.

AIR FRYER TIP: If you have a convection oven–style air fryer, keep the sandwiches as far away from the heating element as possible so that the bread won't burn before the filling gets melty.

PER SERVING (1 SANDWICH): Calories: 232; Fat: 13g; Sodium: 292mg; Carbohydrates: 37g; Fiber: 5g; Sugar: 5g; Protein: 7g

CRISPY SPRING ROLLS

30 MINUTES

Crunch! That's the first thing you'll notice when you bite into one of these crispy spring rolls. Then you'll realize how light and flavorful the filling is, with a slight hint of lime and peanut. When you're shopping for your spring roll wrappers, be sure to check the ingredients, as many of them contain eggs. Also be on the lookout for no-fat and low-sodium versions.

MAKES 8 spring rolls
PREP TIME: 10 minutes
COOK TIME: 17 minutes

2 tablespoons natural peanut butter
2 tablespoons freshly squeezed lime juice
1 tablespoon No-Salt Hot Sauce (page 108)
4 scallions, both white and green parts, thinly sliced
½ (16-ounce) bag coleslaw mix
8 spring roll wrappers
Nonstick cooking spray

1. In a large bowl, mix together the peanut butter, lime juice, and hot sauce. Then add the scallions and coleslaw mix and toss to coat completely.

2. Lay out a spring roll wrapper with one of the corners facing you. Scoop one-eighth of the filling (about ½ cup) onto the corner nearest you. Fold the corner up over the filling, and gently push the filling back toward you to compact it. Then fold in the sides and continue rolling the wrapper away from you. Repeat with the remaining wrappers.

3. Place the rolls, seam-side down, in the air fryer basket or on the rack and lightly spray them with oil. Bake at 350°F for 17 minutes, or until browned and crispy. Flip the rolls over halfway through cooking. Enjoy warm.

SOS-FREE: Instead of spraying the spring rolls with oil, you can brush on some aquafaba so the wrappers won't dry out.

AIR FRYER TIP: We only spray our spring rolls with oil once before cooking, but you can also spray them after you've flipped them over for extra crispiness.

PER SERVING (2 SPRING ROLLS): Calories: 256; Fat: 5g; Sodium: 291mg; Carbohydrates: 44g; Fiber: 3g; Sugar: 3g; Protein: 9g

FRY 400°F

FISHLESS TACOS

30 MINUTES • GLUTEN-FREE

Tofu and dulse granules make a great substitute for fish in these tasty little tacos. We like to use super-firm tofu for this recipe because it doesn't need to be pressed. However, if you have trouble finding it, you can use extra-firm tofu instead and carefully press out as much of the liquid as possible before cutting it.

SERVES 2
PREP TIME: 15 minutes
COOK TIME: 15 minutes

4 tablespoons freshly squeezed lime juice, divided

2 tablespoons No-Salt Hot Sauce (page 108), divided

½ teaspoon dulse granules

½ teaspoon ground cumin

½ (16-ounce) block super-firm tofu

1½ cups shredded red cabbage

2 scallions, both white and green parts, finely sliced

1½ tablespoons vegan mayonnaise

2 tablespoons finely chopped fresh cilantro

4 (5- or 6-inch) corn tortillas

SOS-FREE: To make this recipe SOS-free, leave the mayo out of the slaw and instead top each taco with 1 tablespoon of unsweetened plain coconut yogurt.

1 In a medium bowl, mix together 2 tablespoons lime juice, 1 tablespoon hot sauce, the dulse granules, and the cumin until well combined. Set aside.

2 Cut the tofu into 4 equal slices. Dip both sides of each slice into the sauce and place them in the air fryer basket or on the rack in a single layer. Spoon half of the leftover sauce over the tofu.

3 Fry at 400°F for 6 minutes. Then flip the tofu over and spoon the remaining sauce over the top. Continue frying for 6 minutes more.

4 Meanwhile, make the slaw. In a medium bowl, mix together the red cabbage, scallions, vegan mayonnaise, cilantro, remaining 2 tablespoons lime juice, and remaining 1 tablespoon hot sauce until well combined.

5 Remove the tofu from the air fryer. As the tofu is cooling, warm up the tortillas in the air fryer. Place the tortillas in the air fryer basket or on the rack in a single layer and fry at 400°F for 2 to 3 minutes.

6 When the tofu has cooled slightly, cut each slab into ½-inch-thick strips.

7 Remove the tortillas from the air fryer and spoon one-quarter of the slaw onto each tortilla. Then top each with one-quarter of the tofu strips. Enjoy warm.

PER SERVING (2 TACOS): Calories: 290; Fat: 12g; Sodium: 124mg; Carbohydrates: 36g; Fiber: 5g; Sugar: 5g; Protein: 16g

TOASTED BEAN BURRITOS

30 MINUTES

The air fryer takes burritos to the next level by making the tortillas extra crispy. To avoid the extra salt and oil, we made our own "unfried" beans with kidney beans instead of using store-bought refried beans. We recommend enjoying these burritos with our No-Cheese Sauce (page 109).

MAKES 2 burritos
PREP TIME: 10 minutes
COOK TIME: 10 minutes

1 (15.5-ounce) can dark red kidney beans, drained and rinsed
1 tablespoon Mild Taco Seasoning (page 107)
2 tablespoons freshly squeezed lime juice
2 (10-inch) flour tortillas
¼ cup low-sodium salsa
2 scallions, both white and green parts, thinly sliced
1 tablespoon No-Salt Hot Sauce (page 108)

1 In a medium bowl, use a fork to mash the kidney beans. Then add the taco seasoning and lime juice and mix until well combined. Set aside.

2 Lay out the tortillas on a flat surface. Spoon half of the salsa into the middle of each tortilla, followed by the scallions and the bean mixture. Then drizzle half of the hot sauce over the filling on each tortilla.

3 To roll up the burrito, fold in the sides of the tortilla. Then fold up the bottom one-third of the way and continue to roll up until you run out of tortilla. Repeat with the second tortilla.

4 Place the burritos, seam-side down, in the air fryer basket or on the rack and grill at 400°F for 10 minutes, or until the tortillas are crispy. Be sure to carefully flip the burritos over halfway through cooking. Enjoy warm.

SUBSTITUTE IT: Feel free to use a store-bought taco seasoning or hot sauce in place of ours. And for a different flavor, try using pinto or black beans instead of the kidney beans.

SOS-FREE: To make this SOS-free, swap out the low-sodium salsa for your own homemade salsa and use corn tortillas instead of flour, which would also make this recipe gluten-free. To prevent tearing when rolling, wrap the tortillas in aluminum foil and warm them in the air fryer at 400°F for 2 minutes before using.

PER SERVING (1 BURRITO): Calories: 398; Fat: 5g; Sodium: 423mg; Carbohydrates: 72g; Fiber: 13g; Sugar: 5g; Protein: 18g

CHICKENLESS FILLETS

30 MINUTES • WFPB

We use vital wheat gluten to give these seitan fillets a meat-like texture. You can enjoy them in place of a grilled chicken breast; they taste wonderful on a salad or in pasta dishes. But our favorite way to eat these fillets is on a hot chickenless sandwich with lettuce, tomatoes, onions, and our Super Ranch Dressing (page 110).

MAKES 3 fillets
PREP TIME: 10 minutes
COOK TIME: 16 minutes

¾ cup canned chickpeas, drained and rinsed
¼ cup roasted red peppers
1 tablespoon No-Salt Hot Sauce (page 108)
1 tablespoon balsamic vinegar
¼ cup water
1 tablespoon No-Salt Spice Blend (page 106)
½ teaspoon ground sage
½ cup vital wheat gluten

1 In a blender, blend the chickpeas, roasted red peppers, hot sauce, balsamic vinegar, and water until smooth. Set aside.

2 In a medium bowl, mix together the spice blend, sage, and vital wheat gluten. Then add the chickpea mixture to the bowl and mix until well combined.

3 Divide the mixture into 3 (½-inch-thick) fillets and place them in the air fryer basket or on the rack.

4 Bake at 360°F for 16 minutes, or until the fillets are lightly browned. Be sure to flip the fillets over halfway through cooking. Enjoy warm or cold.

AIR FRYER TIP: Lightly spray the fillets with oil before and midway through cooking for a crispier texture. Or to keep this recipe SOS-free, brush the fillets with aquafaba before and halfway through cooking.

PER SERVING (1 FILLET): Calories: 136; Fat: 1g; Sodium: 16mg; Carbohydrates: 16g; Fiber: 3g; Sugar: 3g; Protein: 14g

SMOKY BEAN BURGERS

30 MINUTES • WFPB

These healthy bean burgers get their smoky flavor from liquid smoke, which can be found in most grocery stores near the barbecue sauce. Look for one that contains only water and smoke concentrate. For maximum deliciousness, we recommend serving these burgers on a toasted bun with lettuce, tomato, onion, and our No-Cheese Sauce (page 109).

MAKES 4 burgers
PREP TIME: 10 minutes
COOK TIME: 15 minutes

1 (15.5-ounce) can dark red kidney beans, drained and rinsed
¼ cup canned diced tomatoes
2 tablespoons balsamic vinegar
2 tablespoons No-Salt Hot Sauce (page 108)
1 tablespoon No-Salt Spice Blend (page 106)
1 teaspoon liquid smoke
⅓ cup vital wheat gluten

1 In a medium bowl, use a fork to mash the kidney beans. Add the diced tomatoes with their juices, balsamic vinegar, hot sauce, spice blend, and liquid smoke to the bowl and mix until well combined. Then add the vital wheat gluten and mix again.

2 Divide the mixture into 4 equal patties and place them in the air fryer basket or on the rack in a single layer.

3 Bake at 360°F for 15 minutes, or until the patties are crispy. Flip the patties over halfway through cooking. Serve warm.

SUBSTITUTE IT: If you don't like kidney beans, swap them out for 1 (15.5-ounce) can of pinto or black beans.

PER SERVING (1 BURGER): Calories: 123; Fat: 0g; Sodium: 10mg; Carbohydrates: 18g; Fiber: 5g; Sugar: 2g; Protein: 11g

ZUCCHINI LASAGNA ROLL-UPS, PAGE 79

CHAPTER 6

MAIN DISHES

SPICY PINEAPPLE-CAULIFLOWER STIR-FRY

GLUTEN-FREE • WFPB

Caramelized pineapple is the perfect complement to the medium-spicy hot sauce in this dish. We like to use the stems and core of the cauliflower and save the florets for our Sweet and Spicy Cauliflower Wings (page 60). We recommend serving this stir-fry over rice to complete the meal.

SERVES 2
PREP TIME: 15 minutes
COOK TIME: 27 minutes

¼ cup No-Salt Hot Sauce (page 108)

¼ cup freshly squeezed lime juice

2 teaspoons No-Salt Spice Blend (page 106)

½ head cauliflower, cut into bite-size pieces

½ pineapple, cut into bite-size chunks

2 medium carrots, thinly sliced

1 cup frozen peas, thawed

2 scallions, green parts only, finely chopped

SUBSTITUTE IT: If you're not a fan of cauliflower, swap it out for another cruciferous veggie, such as broccoli. And feel free to use your favorite hot sauce in place of the No-Salt Hot Sauce.

1 In a large bowl, mix together the hot sauce, lime juice, and spice blend. Add the cauliflower, pineapple, and carrots and toss to coat.

2 Place the vegetable mixture in the air fryer basket or on the rack, leaving behind in the mixing bowl any sauce that wasn't absorbed. Fry at 400°F for 12 minutes. Shake up the air fryer basket or stir the veggies and fry for an additional 12 minutes, or until the veggies are cooked through.

3 Meanwhile, put the peas and scallions in the bowl with the remaining sauce. Toss to coat. Place the peas and scallions in a small pan and set aside.

4 Remove the veggies from the air fryer and transfer them to a serving bowl. Fry the peas and scallions for 3 minutes.

5 Add the peas and scallions to the serving bowl and stir. Serve warm.

AIR FRYER TIP: Remember not to overcrowd your air fryer basket or rack. Depending on the size of your air fryer, you may need to cook this recipe in several batches.

PER SERVING (½ OF THE RECIPE): Calories: 169; Fat: 1g; Sodium: 93mg; Carbohydrates: 37g; Fiber: 9g; Sugar: 20g; Protein: 8g

SPINACH MARGHERITA PIZZA

Margherita pizza is traditionally made with fresh basil, but we like to make ours with baby spinach instead. The creamy cashew mozzarella is a delicious plant-based replacement for fresh dairy mozzarella. Make sure you look for a tomato sauce with low oil and no added salt or sugar.

MAKES 4 mini pizzas
PREP TIME: 15 minutes
COOK TIME: 32 minutes

½ cup jarred tomato sauce
1 teaspoon dried oregano
1 teaspoon granulated garlic
1 pound frozen pizza
   dough, thawed
1 cup baby spinach
½ cup Cashew Mozzarella
   (page 114)

1 In a small bowl, mix together the tomato sauce, oregano, and granulated garlic until well combined. Set aside.

2 Divide the pizza dough evenly into 4 balls and roll out each ball into a 6-inch round pizza crust.

3 Place one pizza crust directly in the air fryer basket or on the rack. Spread one-quarter of the sauce mixture all over the crust, leaving a 1-inch edge all around. Cover the sauce with one-quarter of the baby spinach. Finally, top the pizza with small dollops of the cashew mozzarella and spread it around a little bit.

4 Grill at 400°F for 8 minutes, or until the pizza is lightly browned and the crust is crispy. Repeat with each of the remaining pizzas and serve warm.

SUBSTITUTE IT: Feel free to use your own fresh pizza dough in place of the frozen. Additionally, the possibilities for toppings are endless. Jazz up your pizza with mushrooms, broccoli, or eggplant. And if you're a fan of Hawaiian pizza, pineapple caramelizes perfectly in the air fryer.

AIR FRYER TIP: We find that the pizza comes out the crispiest when you cook it right in the air fryer basket or on the rack. But you can save time by using perforated mini pizza pans to prep your pies while the first one is cooking.

PER SERVING (1 MINI PIZZA): Calories: 322; Fat: 5g; Sodium: 427mg; Carbohydrates: 58g; Fiber: 4g; Sugar: 7g; Protein: 12g

GLUTEN-FREE WHITE PIZZA

30 MINUTES • GLUTEN-FREE • WFPB

This gluten-free quinoa crust is so quick and easy to make and doesn't require any oil or salt. We love a tasty white pizza, but if you prefer, you can make it more traditional with a tomato sauce and our Cashew Mozzarella (page 114). Don't forget to add your favorite toppings.

SERVES 2
PREP TIME: 15 minutes
COOK TIME: 10 minutes

¾ cup quinoa flour
½ teaspoon dried basil
½ teaspoon dried oregano
1 tablespoon apple
   cider vinegar
½ cup water
⅓ cup Almond Ricotta
   (page 115)
⅔ cup frozen
   broccoli, thawed
½ teaspoon
   granulated garlic

SUBSTITUTE IT: If you don't want to make this gluten-free, you can use a wheat-based pizza dough instead of the quinoa crust. You won't have to prebake the crust, so just put your toppings on it and grill at 400°F for 8 minutes.

1 In a medium bowl, mix together the quinoa flour, basil, oregano, apple cider vinegar, and water until well combined. Set aside.

2 Cut a piece of parchment paper to fit your air fryer basket or rack and transfer the quinoa mixture to the parchment paper. To form the crust, cover the mixture with another piece of parchment and press down on it to flatten it out to the edges of the bottom piece of parchment. Then discard the top layer of parchment.

3 Transfer the crust, along with the bottom piece of parchment, to the air fryer. Bake at 350°F for 5 minutes. Then carefully flip the crust over in the air fryer and peel off the parchment paper.

4 Spread the almond ricotta evenly over the crust, leaving a ½-inch edge all around. Then place the broccoli over it and sprinkle the granulated garlic on top.

5 Grill at 400°F for 5 minutes, or until the toppings are lightly browned. Serve immediately.

AIR FRYER TIP: If you have a small air fryer, you can make 2 smaller pizzas using the ingredients listed.

PER SERVING (½ PIZZA): Calories: 256; Fat: 11g; Sodium: 15mg; Carbohydrates: 33g; Fiber: 7g; Sugar: 1g; Protein: 12g

STUFFED ROASTED SWEET POTATOES

GLUTEN-FREE • WFPB

This hearty dish is the embodiment of the phrase "Teamwork makes the dream work." Each ingredient is tasty on its own, but when they are combined like this, they are perfection.

SERVES 2
PREP TIME: 10 minutes
COOK TIME: 30 minutes

2 medium sweet potatoes
1 (15.5-ounce) can black beans, drained and rinsed
2 scallions, both white and green parts, finely sliced
1 tablespoon No-Salt Hot Sauce (page 108)
1 teaspoon Mild Taco Seasoning (page 107)
2 tablespoons freshly squeezed lime juice
¼ cup Lemon-Tahini Dressing (page 11)

1 Place the whole sweet potatoes in the air fryer basket or on the rack and roast at 400°F for 30 minutes.

2 Meanwhile, in a medium bowl, combine the black beans, scallions, hot sauce, taco seasoning, and lime juice. Set aside.

3 Carefully remove the sweet potatoes from the air fryer and cut each lengthwise, two-thirds of the way through.

4 Fill each sweet potato with half of the bean mixture. Then drizzle half of the lemon-tahini dressing over each. Serve warm.

SUBSTITUTE IT: Our No-Salt Hot Sauce packs a medium heat, so swap it out for your favorite if you want a different level of spiciness.

AIR FRYER TIP: Try to use 2 sweet potatoes that are relatively close in size so they'll cook in the same amount of time. If you're using larger sweet potatoes, you may need to cook them for up to 10 minutes longer.

PER SERVING (1 STUFFED SWEET POTATO): Calories: 347; Fat: 5g; Sodium: 83mg; Carbohydrates: 63g; Fiber: 17g; Sugar: 8g; Protein: 15g

EGGPLANT PARM

Eggplant dishes are typically very high in oil because the eggplant sucks it all up like a sponge. However, this eggplant parm is super crispy and delicious without any added oil. We use four of our own staple ingredients in this recipe, which are all SOS-free, but you can save some time by using store-bought substitutes. We like to round out this meal by serving the eggplant over pasta or on a toasted roll.

SERVES 4
PREP TIME: 20 minutes
COOK TIME: 20 minutes

¾ cup chickpea flour
½ cup unsweetened plain plant-based milk
3 tablespoons freshly squeezed lemon juice
1 tablespoon No-Salt Hot Sauce (page 108)
2 teaspoons No-Salt Spice Blend (page 106)
1½ cups panko bread crumbs
1 medium eggplant
2 cups jarred tomato sauce, divided
½ cup Almond Ricotta (page 115)
⅓ cup Cashew Mozzarella (page 114)

1 In a medium bowl, mix the chickpea flour, plant-based milk, lemon juice, hot sauce, and spice blend until well combined. Set aside. Pour the bread crumbs onto a plate and set aside.

2 Trim and discard the ends of the eggplant. Then cut the eggplant into ½-inch-thick slices. Dip each eggplant slice into the batter, shaking off any excess. Then dip the slices into the bread crumbs to completely coat them.

3 Place the eggplant slices in the air fryer basket or on the rack in a single layer. Fry at 400°F for 10 minutes, flipping over halfway through cooking.

4 Meanwhile, spread 2 tablespoons of the tomato sauce around the bottom of a baking pan.

5 Let the eggplant cool slightly. Place a single layer of the eggplant in the pan with the tomato sauce, spread a thin layer of almond ricotta on top of each slice, and spoon some more tomato sauce over the top. Continue creating these layers of sauce, eggplant, and almond ricotta until all of the eggplant is in the pan. Spoon the remaining tomato sauce over the top. Then place dollops of the cashew mozzarella on top and spread them out a little.

6 Place the pan in the air fryer and bake at 350°F for 10 minutes, or until the eggplant is heated through and the cashew mozzarella is lightly browned. Serve warm.

SOS-FREE: This dish is already low in sodium, but you can make it completely SOS-free by making your own tomato sauce instead of buying it and leaving out the bread crumbs, which would also make it gluten-free.

AIR FRYER TIP: Leave a little space between the eggplant slices during the first round of cooking so the hot air will be able to circulate all the way around them. If desired, lightly spray the coated eggplant with oil before the first round of cooking for extra crispiness. If your tomato sauce is too thick to begin with, add a little water to it because the air fryer tends to dry out sauces during cooking.

PER SERVING (¼ OF THE RECIPE): Calories: 342; Fat: 13g; Sodium: 220mg; Carbohydrates: 47g; Fiber: 11g; Sugar: 13g; Protein: 16g

STUFFED BELL PEPPERS

GLUTEN-FREE • WFPB

This was always a favorite meal of our beloved Gramps, but his version included chopped meat and rice. We've put our own spin on it here, using all plant-based ingredients. In place of the chopped meat, we like to use textured vegetable protein, which is made from soy and is high in protein and fiber.

SERVES 3
PREP TIME: 10 minutes
COOK TIME: 30 minutes

1½ cups textured vegetable protein
1 tablespoon No-Salt Spice Blend (page 106)
3 tablespoons freshly squeezed lemon juice
1 cup boiling water
¾ cup No-Cheese Sauce (page 109)
½ cup canned diced tomatoes
¾ cup quinoa flour
2 tablespoons dried parsley
2 tablespoons No-Salt Hot Sauce (page 108)
¼ teaspoon freshly ground black pepper
3 large bell peppers

1 In a medium bowl, combine the textured vegetable protein, spice blend, lemon juice, and boiling water. Then add the no-cheese sauce, diced tomatoes with their juices, quinoa flour, parsley, hot sauce, and black pepper and mix until well combined. Set aside.

2 Using a sharp knife, carefully cut all the way around the top of a bell pepper, as if you are cutting out a lid. Do not cut through the core. Twist the top of the pepper and pull out the core and all of the seeds without breaking the rest of the pepper. Repeat with the other 2 bell peppers.

3 Divide the stuffing mixture evenly among the 3 bell peppers, filling them all the way to the top.

4 Cover each bell pepper with a 6-inch square of aluminum foil and flip it upside down. Fold the corners of the aluminum foil up against the sides of each pepper.

5 Place the bell peppers in the air fryer basket or on the rack and roast at 375°F for 30 minutes, or until the peppers are soft and tender. Let cool slightly before unwrapping and flipping the peppers over. Enjoy warm.

SUBSTITUTE IT: For a slightly different flavor, you can substitute lime juice for the lemon juice. You can also swap out the dried parsley for fresh cilantro.

PER SERVING (1 STUFFED PEPPER): Calories: 380; Fat: 4g; Sodium: 33mg; Carbohydrates: 52g; Fiber: 16g; Sugar: 10g; Protein: 36g

BAKED MAC AND CHEEZ

30 MINUTES • 5 INGREDIENTS

This creamy mac and cheez is so quick and easy to prepare, you'll want to whip up a second batch immediately. We like to use elbow macaroni for this recipe because it holds more of the sauce, but you can use any type of pasta you like, including gluten-free or whole-wheat. To figure out how many minutes your pasta needs to cook in the air fryer, always check the cooking instructions on the pasta box. Subtract 1 minute from the lower end of the al dente range.

SERVES 3
PREP TIME: 10 minutes
COOK TIME: 15 minutes

1 cup No-Cheese Sauce
   (page 109)
1 cup unsweetened plain
   plant-based milk
½ cup Cashew Mozzarella
   (page 114)
1 tablespoon
   nutritional yeast
½ (16-ounce) box uncooked
   elbow macaroni
3 to 4 cups boiling water

1 In a small metal baking pan, mix together the no-cheese sauce, plant-based milk, cashew mozzarella, and nutritional yeast until well combined. Cover the pan with aluminum foil, place it in the air fryer, and bake at 400°F for 6 minutes.

2 Meanwhile, place the uncooked macaroni in another metal baking pan. Pour just enough boiling water over the macaroni to completely cover it. Then cover the pan tightly with aluminum foil.

3 Place the macaroni pan in the air fryer, on top of the pan with the sauce in it. Bake for 6 minutes.

4 Take both pans out of the air fryer and carefully remove the foil from each. Drain the macaroni in a colander and return it to the pan. Pour the sauce over the macaroni and stir to coat. Bake, uncovered, for 3 minutes, or until the mac and cheez is heated through and bubbly. Serve immediately.

AIR FRYER TIP: We recommend using metal or glass pans for this recipe. Silicone pans won't get hot enough to cook the sauce or pasta evenly. If you have a small air fryer, cook your pasta first. Then rinse it in cold water and set it aside while the sauce is cooking.

PER SERVING (⅓ OF THE RECIPE): Calories: 379; Fat: 5g; Sodium: 63mg; Carbohydrates: 66g; Fiber: 4g; Sugar: 3g; Protein: 17g

OIL-FREE PASTA BAKE

30 MINUTES

We like to use penne pasta for this dish, but feel free to use other shapes of pasta or gluten-free varieties like chickpea or lentil pasta. Avoid using spaghetti or linguine, which need to be stirred during cooking. To figure out how many minutes your pasta should cook in the air fryer, always check the cooking instructions on the pasta box. Subtract 1 minute from the lower end of the al dente range.

SERVES 3
PREP TIME: 10 minutes
COOK TIME: 18 minutes

1½ cups canned diced
    tomatoes
2 large garlic cloves, minced
1 teaspoon granulated onion
¾ teaspoon dried basil
¾ teaspoon dried oregano
2 tablespoons freshly
    squeezed lemon juice
½ (16-ounce) box uncooked
    penne pasta
3 to 4 cups boiling water

1 In a small metal baking pan, mix the diced tomatoes with their juices, garlic, granulated onion, basil, oregano, and lemon juice. Cover tightly with aluminum foil and bake at 400°F for 6 minutes.

2 Meanwhile, place the uncooked pasta in another metal baking pan. Pour just enough boiling water over the pasta to completely cover it. Then cover the pan tightly with aluminum foil.

3 Place the pasta pan in the air fryer, on top of the pan with the sauce in it. Bake for 9 minutes.

4 Take both pans out of the air fryer and carefully remove the foil from each. Drain the pasta in a colander and return it to the pan. Pour the sauce over the pasta and stir to coat. Re-cover the pan with foil and bake for 3 minutes, or until the pasta and sauce are heated through and bubbly. Stir thoroughly before serving.

AIR FRYER TIP: We recommend using metal or glass pans for this recipe. Silicone pans won't get hot enough to cook the sauce or pasta evenly. If you have a small air fryer, cook your pasta first. Then rinse it in cold water and set it aside while the sauce is cooking.

PER SERVING (⅓ OF THE RECIPE): Calories: 307; Fat: 2g; Sodium: 24mg; Carbohydrates: 62g; Fiber: 5g; Sugar: 6g; Protein: 11g

ZUCCHINI LASAGNA ROLL-UPS

GLUTEN-FREE

These lasagna roll-ups are a fresh and light take on a dish that is traditionally very heavy and full of oil. Thinly sliced zucchini is a wonderfully healthy substitute for lasagna noodles. You can use a mandoline to cut your zucchini slices to save some prep time and ensure more uniform slices.

SERVES 2
PREP TIME: 15 minutes
COOK TIME: 25 minutes

2 medium zucchini
2 tablespoons freshly squeezed lemon juice
1½ cups Almond Ricotta (page 115)
1 tablespoon No-Salt Spice Blend (page 106)
2 cups jarred tomato sauce, divided
⅓ cup Cashew Mozzarella (page 114)

SOS-FREE: We love the convenience of using jarred tomato sauce, but you can make this dish SOS-free by using your own homemade tomato sauce.

1 Using a sharp knife, trim the ends of the zucchini. Then carefully cut each zucchini lengthwise into about ¼-inch slices. Place the slices in the air fryer basket or on the rack in a single layer and sprinkle them with the lemon juice. Roast at 400°F for 5 minutes, or until the zucchini is pliable.

2 Meanwhile, in a small bowl, mix the almond ricotta and the spice blend together. Set aside. Then spread 2 tablespoons of the tomato sauce on the bottom of a small baking pan.

3 Let the zucchini cool slightly before spreading 1 to 2 tablespoons of the almond ricotta mixture onto one side of each slice. Roll up each slice tightly and place them, spiral-side up, in the pan with the tomato sauce. Spoon any remaining almond ricotta over the roll-ups. Then pour the remaining tomato sauce over the top.

4 Evenly space out dollops of the cashew mozzarella over the top of the dish and spread them out slightly.

5 Place the pan in the air fryer and bake at 360°F for 20 minutes, or until the cashew mozzarella is nicely browned. Serve immediately.

AIR FRYER TIP: You don't need to leave any space in between the zucchini roll-ups in the pan because this is a casserole dish.

PER SERVING (½ OF THE RECIPE): Calories: 685; Fat: 51g; Sodium: 50mg; Carbohydrates: 44g; Fiber: 18g; Sugar: 17g; Protein: 30g

FULLY LOADED QUESADILLAS

30 MINUTES

This fun twist of stacking the quesadilla doesn't just create a beautiful presentation; it will also guarantee you get a bit of each ingredient in every bite. And the chewy texture of the super-firm tofu makes it a wonderful replacement for chicken. You can also make this gluten-free and WFPB by using corn tortillas.

MAKES 4 quesadillas
PREP TIME: 10 minutes
COOK TIME: 17 minutes

1 (16-ounce) block
   super-firm tofu
2 tablespoons rice vinegar
1 tablespoon Mild Taco
   Seasoning (page 107)
1 ripe avocado, pitted
4 scallions, both white and
   green parts, finely sliced
2 tablespoons freshly
   squeezed lemon juice
4 (10-inch) flour tortillas
¼ cup No-Salt Hot Sauce
   (page 108)
½ cup No-Cheese Sauce
   (page 109)
1½ cups cherry or grape
   tomatoes, halved

1 Cut the tofu into 4 equal slabs. Set aside.

2 In a small bowl, combine the rice vinegar and taco seasoning. Rub the mixture on both sides of each tofu slab. Place the tofu in the air fryer basket or on the rack and fry at 400°F for 12 minutes, or until the tofu is lightly crisped. Be sure to flip the tofu over halfway through cooking.

3 Meanwhile, in a medium bowl, mash the avocado and mix it with the scallions and lemon juice. Set aside.

4 Let the tofu cool slightly before cutting each slab into ½-inch strips.

5 Place a tortilla on a flat surface and make a cut from one edge to the center. Now imagine the circle of the tortilla divided into 4 quadrants. Spread one-quarter of the avocado mixture on one quadrant of the tortilla (next to the cut). Spread 1 tablespoon of the hot sauce on the quadrant next to the avocado, on the other side of the cut. Then spread 2 tablespoons of the no-cheese sauce on the other half of the tortilla. Place one-quarter of the cherry tomatoes and one-quarter of the tofu strips on top of the no-cheese sauce. Starting with the avocado quadrant, fold each quarter over the next one, until you are left with one stacked triangle. Repeat with the rest of the tortillas.

6 Place the quesadillas in the air fryer basket or on the rack and grill at 400°F for 5 minutes, or until the tortillas are crispy. Carefully flip the quesadillas over halfway through cooking. Serve immediately.

SUBSTITUTE IT: We enjoy the sweetness of grape and cherry tomatoes, but feel free to replace them with 2 medium tomatoes, sliced. You can also use your favorite store-bought hot sauce and taco seasoning in place of our staples. And if you don't want to use tofu, swap it out for 1 (15.5-ounce) can of dark red kidney or black beans, rinsed and drained. Just mash the beans and mix them with the taco seasoning.

AIR FRYER TIP: If you're using corn tortillas for this recipe, wrap them in aluminum foil and warm them up in the air fryer at 400°F for 2 minutes while the tofu is cooking so that they won't tear when folding.

PER SERVING (1 QUESADILLA): Calories: 439; Fat: 19g; Sodium: 529mg; Carbohydrates: 50g; Fiber: 7g; Sugar: 5g; Protein: 21g

SWEET AND SPICY SHISH KEBABS

GLUTEN-FREE • WFPB

These shish kebabs are a little taste of summer barbecue all year long. We like to use canned pineapple rings packed in 100-percent juice so that we can use the juice in the sauce. We recommend serving these delectable shish kebabs over rice to round out the meal.

MAKES 8 kebabs
PREP TIME: 20 minutes
COOK TIME: 15 minutes

⅓ cup natural peanut butter
1 (15-ounce) can pineapple rings in 100-percent pineapple juice
2 tablespoons apple cider vinegar
2 tablespoons No-Salt Hot Sauce (page 108)
1 tablespoon No-Salt Spice Blend (page 106)
1 teaspoon ground ginger
1 (16-ounce) block super-firm tofu
1 large red bell pepper, stemmed and seeded
1 medium red onion, peeled
8 whole mushrooms, quartered

1 In a large bowl, mix together the peanut butter, pineapple juice from the can, apple cider vinegar, hot sauce, spice blend, and ginger until well combined. Set aside.

2 Cut the tofu into 32 equal cubes. Then cut the bell pepper into 16 even chunks and the red onion into 8 even wedges. Separate each onion wedge into 2 pieces, for 16 chunks of onion. Cut the pineapple rings into quarters. Add the tofu cubes, bell pepper, red onion, mushrooms, and pineapple pieces to the bowl with the peanut butter mixture and toss gently to coat.

3 Thread the tofu, veggies, and fruit onto 8 skewers in an alternating pattern, so that each skewer has 4 cubes of tofu, 4 pieces of mushroom, 4 pieces of pineapple, 2 chunks of bell pepper, and 2 chunks of red onion.

4 Place the skewers in the air fryer basket or on the rack and grill at 400°F for 15 minutes, or until the veggies are thoroughly cooked and browned. Serve immediately.

SUBSTITUTE IT: If desired, swap out the peanut butter for a different nut butter.

AIR FRYER TIP: We use wooden skewers for this recipe, but metal ones will work, too. Just make sure they will fit in your air fryer.

PER SERVING (2 KEBABS): Calories: 329; Fat: 18g; Sodium: 19mg; Carbohydrates: 30g; Fiber: 4g; Sugar: 22g; Protein: 18g

CURRY IN A HURRY

30 MINUTES • GLUTEN-FREE • WFPB

We love creamy curry dishes, but they are usually high in fat and can be time-consuming to prepare. This curry thickens up quickly in the air fryer, and we've used oat milk instead of coconut milk to make it healthier. We recommend serving this beautiful curry over rice, with a squeeze of lime juice on top.

SERVES 2
PREP TIME: 5 minutes
COOK TIME: 25 minutes

1 cup canned diced
  tomatoes
2 cups unsweetened plain
  oat milk
2 tablespoons freshly
  squeezed lime juice
1 tablespoon No-Salt Spice
  Blend (page 106)
1 tablespoon curry powder
1 teaspoon ground ginger
½ teaspoon ground cumin
1 (12-ounce) bag frozen
  cauliflower, thawed
½ (16-ounce) block
  extra-firm tofu, cubed
¼ cup finely chopped fresh
  cilantro

1 In a large metal baking pan, mix the diced tomatoes with their juices, oat milk, lime juice, spice blend, curry powder, ginger, and cumin together until well combined. Add the cauliflower and tofu cubes to the pan and stir to coat.

2 Place the pan in the air fryer and roast at 375°F for 15 minutes. Then give the curry a good stir and continue roasting for 10 minutes more, or until the curry is bubbly.

3 Remove the pan from the air fryer and stir in the fresh cilantro. Serve warm.

SUBSTITUTE IT: You can use other plant-based milks instead of the oat milk, but we feel that the creaminess of oat milk makes it the closest substitute to coconut milk, which is often used in curries. Since this is a savory dish, make sure your plant-based milk is unsweetened and not vanilla-flavored.

AIR FRYER TIP: We recommend using a metal or glass pan for this recipe. Silicone pans won't get hot enough to cook the food evenly.

PER SERVING (½ OF THE RECIPE): Calories: 253; Fat: 10g; Sodium: 185mg; Carbohydrates: 26g; Fiber: 10g; Sugar: 14g; Protein: 22g

PLANT-BASED PAELLA

GLUTEN-FREE • WFPB

Who would've thought you could cook rice in an air fryer? Surprise: You totally can! This simplified, flavorful, plants-only version of paella replaces the meat with artichoke hearts and chickpeas. Squeeze some more lemon juice over the top before serving for an extra burst of flavor.

SERVES 3
PREP TIME: 15 minutes
COOK TIME: 35 minutes

½ cup roughly chopped
    artichoke hearts
½ cup thinly sliced red
    bell peppers
4 medium white
    mushrooms, thinly sliced
½ cup canned diced
    tomatoes
½ cup canned chickpeas,
    drained and rinsed
3 tablespoons No-Salt Hot
    Sauce (page 108)
2 tablespoons freshly
    squeezed lemon juice
2 tablespoons
    nutritional yeast
1 tablespoon No-Salt Spice
    Blend (page 106)
1 teaspoon dulse granules
1 cup uncooked rice
2 cups boiling water

1 In a metal baking pan, mix together the artichoke hearts, bell peppers, mushrooms, diced tomatoes with their juices, chickpeas, hot sauce, lemon juice, nutritional yeast, spice blend, and dulse granules.

2 Place the pan in the air fryer and roast at 400°F for 10 minutes.

3 Add the uncooked rice and boiling water to the pan and stir. Carefully cover the pan tightly with aluminum foil and roast for 22 minutes. Then remove the foil cover, stir, and continue roasting the paella for an additional 3 minutes, or until the top is crisped.

4 Let the paella cool slightly. Stir once more and serve warm.

SUBSTITUTE IT: If you don't have any dulse granules, you can crumble up and mix in ½ sheet of nori instead.

AIR FRYER TIP: It's important to use a metal or glass pan for this recipe to ensure the rice will cook evenly.

PER SERVING (⅓ OF THE RECIPE): Calories: 318; Fat: 1g; Sodium: 26mg; Carbohydrates: 68g; Fiber: 8g; Sugar: 4g; Protein: 9g

CRISPY TOFU BUDDHA BOWL

This satisfying Buddha bowl is filled to the brim with delicious, healthy ingredients, and it's totally customizable. Feel free to swap out the broccoli and sweet potatoes for your favorite veggies.

SERVES 2
PREP TIME: 15 minutes
COOK TIME: 30 minutes

½ cup uncooked quinoa, rinsed and drained

1 cup boiling water

1 medium sweet potato, peeled and cut into 1-inch cubes

1 (12-ounce) bag frozen broccoli florets, thawed

¾ cup panko bread crumbs

¼ cup chickpea flour

¼ cup No-Salt Hot Sauce (page 108)

½ (16-ounce) block super-firm tofu, cut into 1-inch cubes

¼ cup Lemon-Tahini Dressing (page 111)

2 scallions, green parts only, thinly sliced

1 tablespoon sesame seeds

SOS-FREE: You can swap out the bread crumbs for 2 tablespoons of cornstarch or arrowroot powder. Either option will make this recipe SOS- and gluten-free.

1 Place the quinoa in a small metal baking pan and pour the boiling water over it. Carefully cover the pan tightly with aluminum foil. Place the pan in the air fryer and fry at 400°F for 10 minutes. Remove the pan from the air fryer and set aside. Leave the foil on so the quinoa will continue to steam while you prepare the rest of the meal.

2 Place the sweet potatoes in the air fryer basket or on the rack and fry for 2 minutes. Then add the broccoli and continue to fry for an additional 5 minutes. Shake up the basket and fry for 3 minutes more. Set the sweet potatoes and broccoli aside.

3 Pour the bread crumbs onto a plate. In a medium bowl, mix together the chickpea flour and hot sauce. Add the tofu cubes to the bowl and toss to coat. Then toss the tofu in the bread crumbs until the tofu cubes are fully coated. Place the tofu in the air fryer basket or on the rack in a single layer and fry for 10 minutes, or until crispy.

4 Divide the quinoa, sweet potatoes, and broccoli evenly between 2 bowls. When the tofu is done (but still warm!), add it to the bowls. Drizzle the lemon-tahini dressing over each bowl and sprinkle the scallions and sesame seeds on top. Enjoy warm.

AIR FRYER TIP: It's important to use a metal or glass pan for this recipe to ensure that the quinoa cooks evenly.

PER SERVING (1 BOWL): Calories: 564; Fat: 18g; Sodium: 226mg; Carbohydrates: 76g; Fiber: 14g; Sugar: 11g; Protein: 30g

ROAST 400°F

SHAKSHUKA

GLUTEN-FREE ▪ WFPB

Shakshuka is a North African dish that is traditionally prepared with poached eggs. In this plant-based version, we've replaced the eggs with our creamy Almond Ricotta. We recommend serving this beautiful meal with a side of crusty toasted bread.

SERVES 3
PREP TIME: 10 minutes
COOK TIME: 35 minutes

1 medium red bell
 pepper, seeded and
 finely chopped
1 small red onion,
 finely chopped
1 (28-ounce) can diced
 tomatoes
2 tablespoons bal-
 samic vinegar
1 tablespoon No-Salt Spice
 Blend (page 106)
1 teaspoon ground cumin
1 cup fresh baby spinach
½ cup Almond Ricotta
 (page 115)

1 In a large metal baking pan, mix together the bell pepper, red onion, diced tomatoes with their juices, balsamic vinegar, spice blend, and cumin. Place the pan in the air fryer and roast at 400°F for 25 minutes, stirring after 10 and 20 minutes.

2 Add the baby spinach to the pan and carefully stir it in. Roast for 5 minutes more.

3 Use a spoon to create 3 wells in the shakshuka. Place one-third of the almond ricotta in each well. Roast for an additional 5 minutes; then serve warm.

SUBSTITUTE IT: For a more traditional take, swap out the almond ricotta for our Tofu Scramble Brunch Bowl (page 31). Just leave out the potatoes and peppers.

AIR FRYER TIP: If you have a small air fryer, divide the recipe between 2 smaller pans.

PER SERVING (⅓ OF THE RECIPE): Calories: 168; Fat: 8g; Sodium: 41mg; Carbohydrates: 19g; Fiber: 9g; Sugar: 11g; Protein: 6g

JELLY DONUTS, PAGE 100

DESSERTS

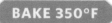

STUFFED BAKED APPLES

30 MINUTES • 5 INGREDIENTS • GLUTEN-FREE • WFPB

This simple but charming dish will fill your whole house with a mouthwatering apple pie smell. We like to use sweet, firm apples for this recipe. For more even cooking, use apples that are similar in size.

SERVES 4
PREP TIME: 5 minutes
COOK TIME: 20 minutes

½ cup Almond Ricotta
   (page 115)
¼ cup raisins
2 apples
½ teaspoon ground
   cinnamon

1 In a small bowl, mix together the almond ricotta and raisins. Set aside.

2 Cut the apples in half, from top to bottom, and remove the core and stem. Sprinkle some cinnamon on each apple half. Then spoon one-quarter of the almond ricotta mixture onto each cut half. Smooth out the filling so that it covers the whole top of the apple.

3 Place the apples in the air fryer basket or on the rack, filling-side up, and bake at 350°F for 7 minutes. Carefully flip the apples over and continue baking for an additional 13 minutes, or until the apples are soft. Serve warm.

AIR FRYER TIP: We recommend using tongs to flip over your apples during cooking, as they'll be quite hot. Flipping the apples keeps the filling from burning and allows the juices from the apple to drip down into the filling. This will also help plump up the raisins.

PER SERVING (½ APPLE): Calories: 167; Fat: 8g; Sodium: 2mg; Carbohydrates: 24g; Fiber: 5g; Sugar: 15g; Protein: 5g

CHICKPEA CHIP COOKIES

30 MINUTES • GLUTEN-FREE

"But these cookies don't taste like chickpeas!" That's what we hear every time we share these cookies with friends and family. The chickpeas are a healthy replacement for the oil in typical chocolate chip cookies without adding a chickpea flavor. To make oat flour, just put rolled oats in a blender and process until you have a fine flour.

MAKES 15 cookies
PREP TIME: 10 minutes
COOK TIME: 13 minutes

1 cup canned chickpeas, drained and rinsed
2 teaspoons vanilla extract
1 teaspoon apple cider vinegar
⅓ cup Date Paste (page 112)
2 tablespoons natural peanut butter
⅓ cup oat flour
½ teaspoon baking powder
¼ cup vegan dark chocolate chips

1 In a food processor, blend the chickpeas, vanilla, and apple cider vinegar until completely smooth.

2 Transfer the mixture to a medium bowl, and add the date paste and peanut butter. Mix until well combined. Sprinkle in the oat flour, baking powder, and chocolate chips and mix to combine.

3 Line the air fryer basket or rack with parchment paper. Scoop the dough into 2-tablespoon balls and place them in the air fryer, leaving some space in between each one. Wet your fingers and flatten each ball of dough into a cookie shape.

4 Bake at 320°F for 13 minutes, or until the cookies are lightly browned. Let the cookies cool slightly before enjoying.

SOS-FREE: To make these cookies SOS-free, use vegan chocolate chips that are sweetened with stevia, or replace the chocolate chips with raisins.

SUBSTITUTE IT: If you don't want to use date paste, you can swap it out for granulated monkfruit sweetener and 2 tablespoons of unsweetened plant-based milk.

AIR FRYER TIP: We like to use a 2-tablespoon cookie scoop to keep the size of our cookies consistent for more even baking.

PER SERVING (3 COOKIES): Calories: 187; Fat: 7g; Sodium: 7mg; Carbohydrates: 25g; Fiber: 5g; Sugar: 10g; Protein: 6g

CHOCOLATE SURPRISE COOKIES

30 MINUTES • GLUTEN-FREE

Surprise! These cookies don't use any flour or processed oils. And instead of sugar, we like to use granulated monkfruit sweetener, which is actually much sweeter than sugar but contains zero calories. Alternatively, you can also sweeten these cookies with coconut sugar, which is less processed and healthier than table sugar.

MAKES 15 cookies
PREP TIME: 15 minutes
COOK TIME: 8 minutes

1 tablespoon ground
  flaxseed
3 tablespoons water
1 teaspoon vanilla extract
1 teaspoon apple
  cider vinegar
⅓ cup natural peanut butter
⅓ cup granulated monkfruit
  sweetener
¼ cup cacao powder
¼ teaspoon baking soda

1 In a medium bowl, mix together the flaxseed, water, vanilla, and apple cider vinegar until well combined. Let sit for 5 minutes.

2 Add the peanut butter and monkfruit sweetener to the bowl and mix again. Sprinkle in the cacao powder and baking soda and mix until well combined. The mixture should be quite thick.

3 Line the air fryer basket or rack with parchment paper. Scoop the dough into 2-tablespoon balls and place them in the air fryer, leaving some space between each.

4 Bake at 300°F for 8 minutes, or until the edges of the cookies start to get dark.

5 Use a fork to flatten each cookie slightly while they're still hot. Let the cookies cool completely before taking them off the parchment paper, as they will still firm and crisp up a bit as they cool.

AIR FRYER TIP: We like to use a 2-tablespoon cookie scoop to keep the size of our cookies consistent for more even baking.

SUBSTITUTE IT: If desired, you can use other nut butters in place of the peanut butter. You can also substitute ¼ cup of Date Paste (page 112) for the granulated monkfruit sweetener; just bake at 320°F for 8 minutes.

PER SERVING (3 COOKIES): Calories: 131; Fat: 9g; Sodium: 73mg; Carbohydrates: 9g; Fiber: 2g; Sugar: 2g; Protein: 5g; Sweetener carbs: 12g

TOASTED ALMOND DELIGHTS

30 MINUTES • GLUTEN-FREE

These delightful almond cookies have been a favorite of our family for many years, but this is the new and improved oil-free version. The banana gives the cookies a nice, cakey center, while the outside is still toasty and crunchy. We especially love to enjoy these cookies with a warm cup of tea or coffee.

MAKES 8 cookies
PREP TIME: 10 minutes
COOK TIME: 18 minutes

1 ripe banana
1 tablespoon almond extract
½ teaspoon ground
    cinnamon
2 tablespoons
    coconut sugar
1 cup almond flour
¼ teaspoon baking soda
8 raw almonds

1 In a medium bowl, use a fork to mash the banana. Add the almond extract, cinnamon, and coconut sugar and mix until well combined. Add the almond flour and baking soda to the bowl and mix again.

2 Line the air fryer basket or rack with parchment paper. Divide the dough into 8 equal balls and flatten each ball to ½ inch thick on the parchment paper. Press 1 almond into the center of each cookie.

3 Bake at 300°F for 12 minutes. Then flip the cookies over and bake for an additional 6 minutes. Let cool slightly before enjoying.

SOS-FREE: To make these cookies SOS-free, swap out the coconut sugar for 2 tablespoons of pure maple syrup.

SUBSTITUTE IT: If you don't have almond extract, you can use vanilla, but the cookies won't taste quite as almondy.

PER SERVING (2 COOKIES): Calories: 204; Fat: 13g; Sodium: 83mg; Carbohydrates: 19g; Fiber: 4g; Sugar: 11g; Protein: 6g

BANANA IN A SLEEPING BAG

30 MINUTES • 5 INGREDIENTS

This dessert version of pigs in a blanket features three of our most-used plant-based staples: dates, peanut butter, and bananas. They are quick and easy to put together, and the spring roll wrappers make a crispy sleeping bag for the soft and warm bananas. When you're shopping for the wrappers, look for ones that are vegan and low-sodium and have zero fat.

MAKES 4 banana rolls
PREP TIME: 10 minutes
COOK TIME: 10 minutes

4 spring roll wrappers
¼ cup Date Paste (page 112)
¼ cup natural peanut butter
2 ripe bananas, halved
    crosswise
1 teaspoon ground
    cinnamon

1 Lay out a spring roll wrapper on a flat surface with one of the corners facing you. Use a spatula to spread 1 tablespoon date paste over the whole wrapper. Then spread 1 tablespoon peanut butter over the date paste.

2 Place one banana half horizontally in the middle of the wrapper and sprinkle some cinnamon over the top. Fold the bottom half of the wrapper over the banana. Then fold in the sides and continue rolling the wrapper away from you. Repeat with the remaining wrappers and ingredients.

3 Place the rolls, seam-side down, in the air fryer basket or on the rack. Roast at 375°F for 10 minutes, or until the wrapper is crispy and lightly browned. Enjoy warm. Store any leftovers in the refrigerator for up to 1 week.

SUBSTITUTE IT: If desired, you can swap out the peanut butter for any other nut or seed butter.

AIR FRYER TIP: You'll know your rolls are done cooking when the banana starts to ooze out of the ends of the wrapper.

PER SERVING (1 BANANA ROLL): Calories: 270; Fat: 9g; Sodium: 187mg; Carbohydrates: 43g; Fiber: 4g; Sugar: 15g; Protein: 8g

BANANA BREAD MUFFINS

30 MINUTES ▪ GLUTEN-FREE ▪ WFPB

These tasty muffins make a wonderful dessert, and if you have any left over, you can eat them for breakfast the next morning. We like to leave little chunks of banana in the batter to keep the muffins moist while baking. And instead of mixing the peanut butter into the batter, we add it on top so the flavor doesn't get lost in the mix. Mmm!

MAKES 6 muffins
PREP TIME: 10 minutes
COOK TIME: 18 minutes

2 ripe bananas
2 tablespoons ground flaxseed
¼ cup unsweetened plant-based milk
1 tablespoon apple cider vinegar
1 tablespoon vanilla extract
½ teaspoon ground cinnamon
2 tablespoons pure maple syrup
½ cup oat flour
½ teaspoon baking soda
3 tablespoons natural peanut butter

1 In a medium bowl, use a fork to mash the bananas, leaving some small chunks intact for texture. Add the flaxseed, plant-based milk, apple cider vinegar, vanilla, cinnamon, and maple syrup to the bowl and mix until well combined. Then add the oat flour and baking soda and mix again.

2 Spoon the batter into 6 cupcake molds, dividing it evenly. Then place 1½ teaspoons peanut butter on top of each muffin. Swirl it around a little bit so that it sticks.

3 Place the muffins in the air fryer and bake at 320°F for 18 minutes, or until the muffins have puffed up and are slightly browned and a toothpick inserted into the center of a muffin comes out clean. Let them cool before enjoying.

SUBSTITUTE IT: If desired, you can swap out the peanut butter for any other nut or seed butter. You can also make these muffins with all-purpose flour instead of oat flour.

AIR FRYER TIP: We like to use silicone cupcake molds for easy cleanup, but a metal muffin pan with a light spritz of oil or parchment cupcake liners will work just fine.

PER SERVING (1 MUFFIN): Calories: 158; Fat: 6g; Sodium: 114mg; Carbohydrates: 22g; Fiber: 3g; Sugar: 10g; Protein: 4g

CARROT CAKE MUFFINS

30 MINUTES • GLUTEN-FREE • WFPB

The cream cheese frosting was always our favorite part of carrot cake, but with these muffins you don't even need it. The pineapple, raisins, and maple syrup are tasty natural sweeteners, and the chopped walnuts on top give these muffins a nice little crunch.

MAKES 6 muffins
PREP TIME: 10 minutes
COOK TIME: 15 minutes

1 cup grated carrot

⅓ cup chopped pineapple

¼ cup raisins

2 tablespoons pure
    maple syrup

⅓ cup unsweetened
    plant-based milk

1 cup oat flour

1 teaspoon ground
    cinnamon

½ teaspoon ground ginger

1 teaspoon baking powder

½ teaspoon baking soda

⅓ cup chopped walnuts

1 In a medium bowl, mix together the carrot, pineapple, raisins, maple syrup, and plant-based milk. Then add the oat flour, cinnamon, ginger, baking powder, and baking soda and mix again until just combined.

2 Divide the batter evenly among 6 cupcake molds. Then sprinkle the chopped walnuts evenly over each muffin. Lightly press the walnuts into the batter so they are partially submerged.

3 Bake at 350°F for 15 minutes, or until the muffins are lightly browned and a toothpick inserted into the center of a muffin comes out clean. Let the muffins cool completely before enjoying.

SUBSTITUTE IT: If you don't like walnuts, you can swap them out for pecans or hemp seed hearts. And if you're not a fan of raisins, you can leave them out and double the pineapple.

AIR FRYER TIP: We like to use silicone cupcake molds for easy cleanup, but a metal muffin pan with a light spritz of oil or parchment cupcake liners will work just fine.

PER SERVING (1 MUFFIN): Calories: 170; Fat: 6g; Sodium: 128mg; Carbohydrates: 27g; Fiber: 3g; Sugar: 11g; Protein: 4g

FUDGY BROWNIES

30 MINUTES • GLUTEN-FREE • WFPB

Brownies typically get their density from using lots of fats. We've replaced the fat in this recipe with pumpkin. To save time, we like to use canned pumpkin, but feel free to use freshly roasted pumpkin instead. If you are using canned pumpkin, make sure pumpkin is the only ingredient, with no additives. (Do not use pumpkin pie filling by accident!) If you'd like these brownies to be extra chocolaty, mix in ¼ cup of vegan dark chocolate chips before baking.

MAKES 4 brownies
PREP TIME: 10 minutes
COOK TIME: 20 minutes

¼ cup canned pumpkin
¼ cup Date Paste (page 112)
¼ cup pure maple syrup
2 tablespoons ground
   flaxseed
1 tablespoon vanilla extract
1 tablespoon water
¼ cup tapioca flour
¼ cup oat flour
½ teaspoon baking powder

1 In a medium bowl, whisk together the pumpkin, date paste, maple syrup, flaxseed, vanilla, and water. Then add the tapioca flour, oat flour, and baking powder to the bowl and mix until combined.

2 Transfer the batter to a 6-inch round cake pan. Wet your spatula and use it to even and smooth out the batter in the pan.

3 Bake at 320°F for 20 minutes, or until a toothpick inserted into the center comes out clean.

4 Let cool before cutting into 4 brownies.

SUBSTITUTE IT: If desired, you can substitute ¼ cup of cooked sweet potato puree for the canned pumpkin. The texture will be similar, but the brownies will be slightly sweeter.

AIR FRYER TIP: We like to use a silicone cake pan for this recipe because we find that they work better for baking in the air fryer. Metal pans are prone to hot spots, which will result in uneven baking.

PER SERVING (1 BROWNIE): Calories: 154; Fat: 2g; Sodium: 7mg; Carbohydrates: 32g; Fiber: 3g; Sugar: 19g; Protein: 2g

BREAD PUDDING

30 MINUTES

This heavenly bread pudding is crunchy on the top and velvety underneath. The date paste adds a caramel flavor with just enough sweetness. You can use any type of bread you'd like, including Ezekiel, which would make this dessert WFPB. Take this dreamy dish to the next level by mixing in ¼ cup of raisins before baking and drizzling some pure maple syrup over the top before serving.

MAKES 4 pieces
PREP TIME: 10 minutes
COOK TIME: 20 minutes

4 slices stale
   whole-grain bread
1 cup unsweetened
   plant-based milk
¼ cup Date Paste (page 112)
2 tablespoons ground
   flaxseed
1 tablespoon vanilla extract
½ teaspoon ground
   cinnamon

1 Cut the slices of bread into even, bite-size pieces and place them in a small cake pan. Set aside.

2 In a medium bowl, whisk together the plant-based milk, date paste, flaxseed, vanilla, and cinnamon. Pour the mixture over the bread and stir to coat.

3 Bake at 320°F for 20 minutes, or until all of the liquid is absorbed and the top is crispy. Cut into 4 pieces and enjoy warm.

AIR FRYER TIP: If you don't have stale bread, you can dry out your slices by baking them in the air fryer at 300°F for 5 to 10 minutes, depending on the type of bread.

PER SERVING (1 PIECE): Calories: 155; Fat: 4g; Sodium: 168mg; Carbohydrates: 23g; Fiber: 4g; Sugar: 8g; Protein: 7g

PUMPKIN CHEEZCAKE

GLUTEN-FREE

This delightful treat combines two of our favorite desserts: pumpkin pie and cheesecake! We used almond ricotta for the "cheese" part, and the coconut yogurt adds the traditional cheesecake tanginess. We recommend chilling this dish overnight before serving, if possible, for the best flavor and texture.

SERVES 4

PREP TIME: 15 minutes, plus 1 hour to chill

COOK TIME: 20 minutes

2 tablespoons natural peanut butter

¼ cup oat flour, plus more as needed

1 tablespoon unsweetened coconut yogurt, plus ½ cup

1 teaspoon coconut sugar, plus 1 tablespoon

¼ cup Almond Ricotta (page 115)

¼ cup canned pumpkin

1 tablespoon vanilla extract

2 tablespoons cornstarch

¼ teaspoon ground cinnamon

> **SOS-FREE:** To make this SOS-free, swap out the coconut sugar for pure maple syrup.

1 In a small bowl, mix together the peanut butter, oat flour, 1 tablespoon coconut yogurt, and 1 teaspoon coconut sugar. If the mixture is too sticky, add another tablespoon oat flour and mix again. To form the crust, use a spatula to press the oat dough onto the bottom and ½ inch up the sides of a small cake pan. Set aside.

2 In a medium bowl, whisk together the almond ricotta, pumpkin, vanilla, cornstarch, cinnamon, remaining ½ cup coconut yogurt, and remaining 1 tablespoon coconut sugar. Pour the mixture over the crust.

3 Bake at 320°F for 20 minutes, or until the cheezcake has puffed up and the top is lightly browned.

4 Let the cheezcake cool completely, during which time it will deflate considerably. Refrigerate for at least 1 hour before cutting into 4 slices to serve.

SUBSTITUTE IT: If desired, you can use any other nut or seed butter in place of the peanut butter. And feel free to use fresh roasted pumpkin or sweet potato instead of the canned pumpkin.

AIR FRYER TIP: We like to use a silicone cake pan for this recipe because we find that they work better for baking in the air fryer. Metal pans are prone to hot spots, which will result in uneven baking.

PER SERVING (1 SLICE): Calories: 203; Fat: 9g; Sodium: 17mg; Carbohydrates: 24g; Fiber: 3g; Sugar: 7g; Protein: 6g

FRY 350°F

JELLY DONUTS

These fluffy donuts are super easy to make. Don't be fooled by the prep time because most of that is just allowing the donuts time to rise. We recommend using a large cookie or biscuit cutter to cut out your donuts. But if you don't have one, a drinking glass will work just fine. Your donuts don't even have to be round, but make sure they're all the same size so they'll cook evenly. Most important, have fun!

MAKES 8 donuts
PREP TIME: 15 minutes, plus 30 minutes to rise
COOK TIME: 8 minutes

¾ cup unsweetened coconut yogurt
2 tablespoons pure maple syrup
1 tablespoon vanilla extract
2 teaspoons active dry yeast
1½ cups all-purpose flour, plus more for rolling and as needed
3 tablespoons unsweetened plant-based milk, divided
½ cup Blueberry Fruit Spread (page 113)

1 In a medium bowl, mix together the coconut yogurt, maple syrup, vanilla, and yeast. Then add the flour and mix again until all of it is incorporated. The dough should be sticky, but if you find that it's too sticky to handle, add 1 to 2 tablespoons of additional flour. Cover the dough and let it rest for 10 minutes.

2 Lay out a piece of parchment paper on a flat surface and sprinkle some flour over it. Place the dough on the parchment and sprinkle a little more flour over it. Use your hands or a rolling pin to flatten the dough to ½ inch thick.

3 Use a 3-inch round cookie cutter to cut out your donuts from the dough. Reroll the scraps and continue cutting out donuts until you run out of dough.

4 Place the donuts in the air fryer basket or on the rack, leaving some space between each. Let the donuts rise for 15 to 20 minutes. Then brush the top of each donut with some of the plant-based milk.

5 Fry at 350°F for 4 minutes. Flip the donuts over and brush the other side with the remaining plant-based milk. Fry for an additional 4 minutes, or until the donuts are puffed up and lightly browned.

6 Let the donuts cool for at least 15 minutes. Using a sharp knife, carefully cut each donut three-quarters of the way through horizontally. Spread 1 tablespoon blueberry fruit spread in the center of each donut. Then gently close each donut and enjoy!

SUBSTITUTE IT: If you're not a fan of blueberries, you can use any type of fruit spread that you'd like. Our Date Paste (page 112) is a delicious alternative filling, but make sure you only use a thin layer, as it is quite sweet.

AIR FRYER TIP: If you want a crispier donut, lightly spray the donuts with oil before and halfway through cooking instead of brushing on the plant-based milk.

PER SERVING (1 DONUT): Calories: 151; Fat: 1g; Sodium: 13mg; Carbohydrates: 31g; Fiber: 2g; Sugar: 8g; Protein: 4g

BLUEBERRY-FILLED LAYER CAKE WITH CHOCOLATE GANACHE

This cute little cake is perfect for small parties or get-togethers. The fruit spread pairs perfectly with the chocolate ganache, and the vanilla cake is light and moist without the use of any eggs or oil.

SERVES 6
PREP TIME: 20 minutes
COOK TIME: 25 minutes

2 tablespoons ground flaxseed

½ cup unsweetened plant-based milk, plus 1 tablespoon

2 tablespoons unsweetened coconut yogurt

¼ cup pure maple syrup

1 tablespoon apple cider vinegar

1 tablespoon vanilla extract

¾ cup all-purpose flour

1 teaspoon baking powder

½ teaspoon baking soda

¼ cup vegan dark chocolate chips

⅓ cup Blueberry Fruit Spread (page 113)

1   In a medium bowl, mix together the flaxseed, ½ cup plant-based milk, coconut yogurt, maple syrup, apple cider vinegar, and vanilla. Then add the flour, baking powder, and baking soda and mix again until just combined. Be careful not to overmix.

2   Pour the cake batter into a 6-inch round cake pan. Then carefully rotate the pan in your hands to distribute the batter so that there is more around the edges than in the middle.

3   Bake at 350°F for 22 minutes, or until a toothpick inserted into the center of the cake comes out clean. Let the cake cool completely in the pan.

4   Carefully turn the cake over onto a plate. Using a sharp knife, cut the cake in half horizontally, so that you have 2 equal layers. Set aside.

5   Place the chocolate chips in a small heat-safe bowl in the air fryer. Bake at 300°F for 3 minutes, or until the chips are melted.

6   Meanwhile, spread the blueberry fruit spread evenly over the top of the bottom layer. Then place the top layer of cake over the fruit spread.

7 Remove the chocolate chips from the air fryer and quickly mix in the remaining 1 tablespoon plant-based milk. Be careful because the bowl will be quite hot.

8 Work quickly to spread the chocolate ganache over the top layer of the cake before the chocolate becomes too hard to spread. Cut the cake into 6 slices and enjoy immediately. Store any leftovers in the refrigerator for up to 1 week.

SOS-FREE: To make this cake SOS-free, use vegan dark chocolate chips that are sweetened with stevia, or spread more fruit spread over the top of the cake instead of the chocolate ganache.

SUBSTITUTE IT: If desired, swap out the Blueberry Fruit Spread for fresh fruit slices. Strawberries, peaches, and pineapple would all taste delicious with this cake.

AIR FRYER TIP. We like to use a silicone cake pan for this recipe because we find that they work better for baking in the air fryer. Metal pans are prone to hot spots, which will result in uneven baking.

PER SERVING (1 SLICE): Calories: 172; Fat: 4g; Sodium: 119mg; Carbohydrates: 30g; Fiber: 3g; Sugar: 14g; Protein: 3g

SUPER RANCH DRESSING, PAGE 110

CHAPTER 8

SEASONINGS, SAUCES, AND STAPLES

NO-SALT SPICE BLEND

30 MINUTES • GLUTEN-FREE • WFPB

This is a basic, tasty, no-salt spice mixture that you can use in tons of different recipes. Whether you're sprinkling it on vegetables, in a pasta sauce, or in a casserole, this blend will enhance the natural flavors of your dish.

MAKES 2 cups
PREP TIME: 5 minutes

¾ cup granulated garlic

¾ cup granulated onion

2 tablespoons dried parsley

2 tablespoons
  dried oregano

2 tablespoons paprika

1 teaspoon white pepper

In an airtight container, combine the granulated garlic, granulated onion, parsley, oregano, paprika, and pepper. Shake until well combined. Store in an airtight container for up to 1 year.

SUBSTITUTE IT: We prefer using granulated garlic and granulated onion for spice blends because they mix in more evenly and have a mellow taste that won't overpower the other spices. If you're using garlic powder and onion powder, use half of the amount listed.

PER SERVING (1 TEASPOON): Calories: 6; Fat: 0g; Sodium: 1mg; Carbohydrates: 1g; Fiber: 0g; Sugar: 0g; Protein: 0g

MILD TACO SEASONING

30 MINUTES • GLUTEN-FREE • WFPB

This is a versatile and mild spice blend that goes a long way in flavoring tacos, French fries, and even kale chips. If you're craving something a little spicier, replace up to half of the chili powder with chipotle, ancho, or Mexican hot chili powder.

MAKES 2 cups
PREP TIME: 5 minutes

1 cup chili powder
4 teaspoons
  granulated garlic
4 teaspoons
  granulated onion
4 teaspoons dried
  Mexican oregano
3 tablespoons paprika
½ cup ground cumin

In an airtight container, combine the chili powder, granulated garlic, granulated onion, oregano, paprika, and cumin. Shake until well combined. Store in an airtight container for up to 1 year.

SUBSTITUTE IT: If you don't have Mexican oregano, which has more of a citrusy flavor, you can use Mediterranean oregano instead. This substitution won't have too much of an impact on the overall flavor of the seasoning.

PER SERVING (1 TEASPOON): Calories: 5; Fat: 0g; Sodium: 10mg; Carbohydrates: 1g; Fiber: 0g; Sugar: 0g; Protein: 0g

NO-SALT HOT SAUCE

30 MINUTES • 5 INGREDIENTS • GLUTEN-FREE • WFPB

Most hot sauces are not SOS-free, but you'd better believe this one is! You can completely customize it to be as spicy or as mild as you want. For a medium-spicy sauce, we use a red bell pepper and Hungarian chile peppers. You can tweak this ratio as you'd like; just make sure your combination of peppers adds up to 1 pound.

MAKES 2½ cups
PREP TIME: 10 minutes
COOK TIME: 15 minutes

1 small garlic bulb
1 red bell pepper
6 Hungarian chile peppers
⅓ cup apple cider vinegar
⅓ cup water
1 Medjool date, pitted

1 Peel the garlic cloves and wrap them together loosely in aluminum foil.

2 Place the garlic and the whole bell pepper and whole chile peppers (stems included) in the air fryer basket or on the rack and roast at 390°F for 15 minutes, or until the skin on the peppers is completely blistered but not burnt. Let the peppers cool slightly before removing the stems and unwrapping the garlic.

3 Place the peppers and garlic in a blender along with the apple cider vinegar, water, and Medjool date. Blend on high until completely smooth.

4 Store in an airtight container in the refrigerator for up to 3 weeks.

SUBSTITUTE IT: If you don't have a Medjool date, you can use 1 tablespoon of maple syrup instead.

PREPARATION TIP: The seeds hold most of the heat in hot peppers, so if you want a milder sauce, remove the seeds when you remove the stems from the peppers.

PER SERVING (2 TABLESPOONS): Calories: 14; Fat: 0g; Sodium: 2mg; Carbohydrates: 3g; Fiber: 0g; Sugar: 2g; Protein: 0g

NO-CHEESE SAUCE

30 MINUTES • GLUTEN-FREE • WFPB

Out of all the recipes in this book, this is our favorite. We use this no-salt "cheese" sauce almost every day, whether it's as a dipping sauce, for mac and "cheese," or drizzled over veggies or Mexican dishes. To keep this recipe easy, we like to use a jarred roasted red pepper. Just make sure it's packed in water, not oil.

MAKES 2½ cups
PREP TIME: 10 minutes

1 large roasted red pepper
¾ cup canned small white beans, drained and rinsed
⅓ cup hemp seed hearts
½ cup unsweetened plain plant-based milk
¼ cup freshly squeezed lemon juice
¼ cup No-Salt Hot Sauce (page 108)
¼ cup nutritional yeast
1 teaspoon granulated garlic
1 teaspoon granulated onion

1 In a blender, blend the roasted red pepper, white beans, hemp seed hearts, plant-based milk, lemon juice, hot sauce, nutritional yeast, granulated garlic, and granulated onion on high until completely smooth.

2 Store in an airtight container in the refrigerator for 1 to 2 weeks.

SUBSTITUTE IT: If you don't have hemp seed hearts, you can use raw cashews or raw sunflower seeds instead.

PER SERVING (¼ CUP): Calories: 52; Fat: 2g; Sodium: 23mg; Carbohydrates: 5g; Fiber: 1g; Sugar: 1g; Protein: 4g

SUPER RANCH DRESSING

30 MINUTES • GLUTEN-FREE • WFPB

This is about to become your new favorite dressing, sauce, and dip. And the good news is it's super healthy. We've replaced the oil that is typically found in most ranch dressings with hemp seed hearts, which are a great source of healthy fats and protein. This dressing should keep for up to 1 week—if you don't eat it all right away.

MAKES 1½ cups
PREP TIME: 10 minutes

½ cup canned small white
  beans, drained and rinsed
¼ cup hemp seed hearts
⅓ cup unsweetened plain
  plant-based milk
2 tablespoons freshly
  squeezed lemon juice
1 tablespoon apple
  cider vinegar
½ teaspoon
  granulated garlic
½ teaspoon
  granulated onion
½ teaspoon dried dill

1 In a blender, blend the white beans, hemp seed hearts, plant-based milk, lemon juice, apple cider vinegar, granulated garlic, granulated onion, and dill on high until completely smooth. Serve chilled.

2 Store in an airtight container in the refrigerator for up to 1 week.

SUBSTITUTE IT: If you don't have hemp seed hearts, you can use raw cashews or raw sunflower seeds instead. Cashews will give the dressing a creamier texture; sunflower seeds will give it an earthier flavor.

PER SERVING (2 TABLESPOONS): Calories: 32; Fat: 1g; Sodium: 3mg; Carbohydrates: 2g; Fiber: 1g; Sugar: 0g; Protein: 2g

LEMON-TAHINI DRESSING

30 MINUTES • GLUTEN-FREE • WFPB

Light and refreshing, this is an all-around wonderful salad dressing or sauce with no oil or salt. This dressing thickens up in the refrigerator, so you may want to mix in a little water to thin it out for a salad. However, in its thicker state, it's perfect for dipping veggies or chips.

MAKES 1¼ cups
PREP TIME: 10 minutes

⅓ cup tahini
3 tablespoons freshly
   squeezed lemon juice
1 tablespoon apple
   cider vinegar
⅔ cup water
1 Medjool date, pitted
1 large garlic clove
⅛ teaspoon pepper

1 In a blender, blend the tahini, lemon juice, apple cider vinegar, water, Medjool date, garlic, and pepper on high until completely smooth.

2 Store in an airtight container in the refrigerator for up to 2 weeks.

SUBSTITUTE IT: We like to add a little sweetness to this dressing to cut down the acidity. If you don't have a Medjool date, you can use 2 tablespoons of pure maple syrup instead.

PER SERVING (2 TABLESPOONS): Calories: 56; Fat: 4g; Sodium: 9mg; Carbohydrates: 4g; Fiber: 1g; Sugar: 2g; Protein: 1g

DATE PASTE

30 MINUTES • 5 INGREDIENTS • GLUTEN-FREE • WFPB

There's a reason people call dates "nature's candy." The natural sweetness of dates makes them a perfect substitute for caramel or sugar in many dishes. Plus, dates are full of fiber and nutrients, including potassium and iron.

MAKES 2 cups
PREP TIME: 10 minutes

25 Medjool dates
1 cup water

1 Remove the pits from the dates. You should be able to squeeze the dates open and easily pull out the pits.

2 In a food processor, blend the dates and the water until completely smooth. You may need to scrape down the sides of the bowl several times with a spatula.

3 Store in an airtight container in the refrigerator for up to 3 weeks.

PREPARATION TIP: If your dates are too hard to squeeze open with your hands or process, soak them in boiling water for 5 minutes to soften them up. Save 1 cup of the soaking water to use for the recipe because it will be more flavorful than fresh water.

PER SERVING (2 TABLESPOONS): Calories: 104; Fat: 0g; Sodium: 0mg; Carbohydrates: 28g; Fiber: 2g; Sugar: 25g; Protein: 1g

BLUEBERRY FRUIT SPREAD

30 MINUTES • 5 INGREDIENTS • GLUTEN-FREE • WFPB

This naturally sweet fruit spread will add a punch of flavor to your favorite breakfasts and desserts without any added sugar. Plus, the chia seeds give this recipe a little kick of fiber and protein. We find that frozen fruit works best in this recipe and has a more concentrated flavor than fresh fruit. We love to use this spread in place of jams and jellies in our PB&J Power Tarts (page 33) and Jelly Donuts (page 100).

MAKES 2 cups
PREP TIME: 10 minutes
COOK TIME: 5 minutes

1 (12-ounce) bag frozen blueberries, thawed
5 Medjool dates, pitted
2 tablespoons chia seeds

1 In a blender, blend the blueberries, Medjool dates, and chia seeds until smooth.

2 Transfer the mixture to a nonstick pan and cook over low heat on the stovetop for 3 to 5 minutes, or until the spread is thick and bubbly. Be careful not to burn it.

3 Let the spread cool. Store in an airtight container in the refrigerator for up to 1 week.

SUBSTITUTE IT: If desired, swap out the blueberries for your favorite fruit. Strawberries, raspberries, blackberries, apricots, and peaches all make delicious fruit spreads.

PER SERVING (2 TABLESPOONS): Calories: 40; Fat: 1g; Sodium: 1mg; Carbohydrates: 9g; Fiber: 2g; Sugar: 7g; Protein: 1g

CASHEW MOZZARELLA

30 MINUTES • GLUTEN-FREE • WFPB

Many store-bought vegan cheeses are oil-based, but this cashew mozzarella uses only whole foods. This is a spreadable "cheese" when cold, but you can also use it immediately after making it, before it cools down, as a cheesy sauce. This recipe is completely SOS-free, but if desired, you can add up to ½ teaspoon of sea salt for some extra flavor.

MAKES 2 cups
PREP TIME: 10 minutes
COOK TIME: 5 minutes

½ cup raw cashews
1¼ cups unsweetened plain
   plant-based milk
2 tablespoons freshly
   squeezed lemon juice
1 tablespoon apple
   cider vinegar
¼ cup tapioca flour
1 tablespoon nutri-
   tional yeast

1 In a blender, blend the cashews, plant-based milk, lemon juice, apple cider vinegar, tapioca flour, and nutritional yeast on high until smooth.

2 Pour the mixture into a nonstick saucepan. Cook over low heat, constantly stirring, for about 5 minutes, or until the mixture gets thick and stretchy.

3 Turn off the heat and transfer the "cheese" to a storage container. Use a spatula to smooth out the surface and let it cool to room temperature. Store in the refrigerator for 1 to 2 weeks.

SUBSTITUTE IT: If you don't have tapioca flour, you can use 2 tablespoons of agar agar powder or ¼ cup of agar agar flakes instead. This will help the "cheese" firm up.

PER SERVING (¼ CUP): Calories: 71; Fat: 4g; Sodium: 14mg; Carbohydrates: 6g; Fiber: 1g; Sugar: 1g; Protein: 3g

ALMOND RICOTTA

30 MINUTES • 5 INGREDIENTS • GLUTEN-FREE • WFPB

This vegan ricotta works wonderfully in both savory and sweet dishes. We like to remove the skins from the almonds for this recipe. You could totally leave them on to save time, but your ricotta will have more of a tan color.

MAKES 2¼ cups
PREP TIME: 30 minutes

2 cups raw almonds
2 tablespoons freshly squeezed lemon juice
1 tablespoon nutritional yeast
1 cup water, plus more as needed

1 Place the almonds in a medium bowl and cover them with boiling water. Let the almonds soak for 10 minutes before draining the water. Then remove the skins from the almonds by pinching them at one end between your thumb and index finger. The almonds should pop right out.

2 In a blender or food processor, blend the almonds, lemon juice, nutritional yeast, and water until smooth.

3 Store in an airtight container in the refrigerator for 1 to 2 weeks.

PREPARATION TIP: If the mixture is too thick and you are having trouble blending it, add a couple more tablespoons of water.

PER SERVING (¼ CUP): Calories: 185; Fat: 16g; Sodium: 0mg; Carbohydrates: 7g; Fiber: 4g; Sugar: 1g; Protein: 8g

PLANT-BASED AIR FRYER CHART

FRESH FRUIT	QUANTITY	TIME	TEMP	NOTES
APPLES	1 to 2 apples	8 to 10 minutes	350°F	Peel and slice. Sprinkle with cinnamon and nutmeg. Shake halfway through cooking.
BANANAS	1 to 2 bananas	4 to 7 minutes	375°F	Peel, slice, and sprinkle with cinnamon if desired. Flip over halfway through cooking.
PEACHES	1 to 2 peaches	10 to 12 minutes	350°F	Cut into wedges. Sprinkle lightly with cinnamon if desired.
PEARS	1 to 2 pears	12 to 14 minutes	350°F	Cut in half. Sprinkle with cinnamon.

FRESH VEGETABLES	QUANTITY	TIME	TEMP	NOTES
ASPARAGUS	½ pound	5 to 8 minutes	400°F	Trim ends. After cooking, toss with lemon juice and seasonings.
BROCCOLI	1 to 2 cups	6 to 8 minutes	400°F	Cut into florets and shake halfway through cooking. Then toss with lemon juice and seasonings.
BRUSSELS SPROUTS	1 to 2 cups	10 to 12 minutes	400°F	Trim bottoms and cut in quarters, spray with olive oil, and sprinkle with seasonings. Shake halfway through cooking.
BUTTERNUT SQUASH	1 small squash	15 to 20 minutes	400°F	Peel, cut into cubes, and toss with lemon juice and seasonings. Shake halfway through cooking.
CARROTS	½ to 1 cup	14 to 16 minutes	375°F	Cut, spray with oil, sprinkle with seasonings and shake halfway through cooking.
CAULIFLOWER FLORETS	1 to 2 cups	12 to 15 minutes	375°F	Spray with olive oil, sprinkle with seasonings and shake halfway through cooking.
CORN ON THE COB	2 ears	8 to 10 minutes	400°F	Spray with oil, sprinkle with seasonings, and flip halfway through cooking.

CONTINUED >>

FRESH VEGETABLES	QUANTITY	TIME	TEMP	NOTES
EGGPLANT	1 medium eggplant	13 to 15 minutes	380°F	Cut into cubes, toss in lemon juice and seasonings, and shake halfway through cooking.
GREEN BEANS	½ to 1 pound	7 to 10 minutes	375°F	Trim ends, toss with lemon juice and seasonings, and shake halfway through cooking.
MUSHROOMS	8 to 12 mushrooms	12 to 15 minutes	400°F	Remove stems, sprinkle both sides with seasonings, and flip over halfway through cooking.
ONIONS	1 large onion	12 to 15 minutes	400°F	Slice, spray lightly with oil, and toss with seasonings. Shake twice throughout cooking.
PEPPERS (BELL)	1 to 2 peppers	10 to 12 minutes	400°F	Cut into strips and toss with lemon juice and seasonings. Shake halfway through cooking.
POTATOES (BAKED)	1 to 2 potatoes	40 minutes	400°F	Poke holes first and cook.
POTATOES (CUBED)	1 to 2 potatoes	10 to 15 minutes	400°F	Toss with lemon juice and seasonings and shake halfway through cooking.
POTATOES (FRIES)	1 to 2 potatoes	12 to 15 minutes	400°F	Toss fries with lemon juice and seasonings and shake halfway through cooking.
SWEET POTATOES (BAKED)	1 to 2 medium sweet potatoes	30 to 35 minutes	400°F	Poke holes first and cook.
SWEET POTATOES (CUBED)	1 to 2 medium sweet potatoes	10 to 12 minutes	400°F	Toss cubes with lemon juice and seasoning and shake halfway through cooking.
SWEET POTATOES (FRIES)	1 to 2 medium sweet potatoes	12 to 15 minutes	380°F	Toss fries with lemon juice and seasonings and shake halfway through cooking.
TOMATOES, CHERRY OR GRAPE	1 pint tomatoes	5 to 8 minutes	400°F	If desired, sprinkle with seasonings after cooking.
ZUCCHINI	2 medium zucchini	10 to 12 minutes	400°F	Cut first, toss with lemon juice and seasonings, and shake halfway through cooking.

MEASUREMENT CONVERSIONS

VOLUME EQUIVALENTS (LIQUID)

US STANDARD	US STANDARD (OUNCES)	METRIC (APPROX.)
2 tablespoons	1 fl. oz.	30 mL
¼ cup	2 fl. oz.	60 mL
½ cup	4 fl. oz.	120 mL
1 cup	8 fl. oz.	240 mL
1½ cups	12 fl. oz.	355 mL
2 cups or 1 pint	16 fl. oz.	475 mL
4 cups or 1 quart	32 fl. oz.	1 L
1 gallon	128 fl. oz.	4 L

OVEN TEMPERATURES

FAHRENHEIT (F)	CELSIUS (C) (APPROX.)
250°	120°
300°	150°
325°	165°
350°	180°
375°	190°
400°	200°
425°	220°
450°	230°

VOLUME EQUIVALENTS (DRY)

US STANDARD	METRIC (APPROX.)
⅛ teaspoon	0.5 mL
¼ teaspoon	1 mL
½ teaspoon	2 mL
¾ teaspoon	4 mL
1 teaspoon	5 mL
1 tablespoon	15 mL
¼ cup	59 mL
⅓ cup	79 mL
½ cup	118 mL
⅔ cup	156 mL
¾ cup	177 mL
1 cup	235 mL
2 cups or 1 pint	475 mL
3 cups	700 mL
4 cups or 1 quart	1 L

WEIGHT EQUIVALENTS

US STANDARD	METRIC (APPROX.)
½ ounce	15 g
1 ounce	30 g
2 ounces	60 g
4 ounces	115 g
8 ounces	225 g
12 ounces	340 g
16 ounces or 1 pound	455 g

RESOURCES

BOOKS

The China Study, Dr. T. Colin Campbell and Dr. Thomas M. Campbell, BenBella Books, 2016

Eat to Live, Dr. Joel Fuhrman, Little, Brown Spark, 2011

How Not to Die, Dr. Michael Greger, Flatiron Books, 2015

How Not to Diet, Dr. Michael Greger, Flatiron Books, 2019

The Plant-Based Solution, Dr. Joel K. Kahn, Sounds True, 2020

The Starch Solution, Dr. John McDougall, Rodale Books, 2013

WEBSITES

Forks Over Knives
ForksOverKnives.com
> *This is the companion website to the groundbreaking 2011 documentary* Forks Over Knives, *which illustrates the connection between a healthy plant-based diet and overall well-being. This website contains numerous plant-based recipes, meal plans, and nutritional information.*

NutritionFacts.org
NutritionFacts.org
> *This is a great resource for those who want to learn more about the science behind plant-based eating. Dr. Michael Greger has posted more than a thousand bite-size, easily digestible videos here that analyze the latest developments in nutritional research.*

VegNews
VegNews.com
> VegNews *is a popular magazine about all things vegan: recipes, travel, product and restaurant reviews, news, lifestyle, and so on. Its website provides lots of articles and resources covering a wide range of vegan topics.*

SHOPPING SITES

Amazon

Amazon.com

When all else fails, there's always Amazon! You will find an enormous selection of air fryers and accessories here. Plus, the Subscribe and Save program can help you save lots of money on your most frequently purchased food items.

Target

Target.com

Target offers a wide variety of air fryers and accessories, both in stores and online. It also carries a decent amount of plant-based ingredients.

Thrive Market

ThriveMarket.com

Thrive Market is a membership-based online retailer where you can buy healthy ingredients and plant-based products at a discount. The website makes shopping easy, as you can filter your searches into different categories, such as vegan, organic, gluten-free, and so on. And as a bonus, for each annual membership purchased, the company will donate one to a family in need.

Vegan Essentials

VeganEssentials.com

This online shop exclusively sells vegan products, so you won't have to worry about checking ingredient labels as you shop. It offers a wide variety of ingredients, meat and cheese replacements, sweets, and snacks.

REFERENCES

Almekinder, Elisabeth. "6 Ways to Improve Gut Health." *Blue Zones*. Accessed January 19, 2021. BlueZones.com/2019/04/6-ways-to-improve-gut-health.

Bjarnadottir, Adda. "Why Refined Carbs Are Bad for You." *Healthline*. June 4, 2017. Healthline.com/nutrition/why-refined-carbs-are-bad.

Harvard Health Publishing. "Why Nutritionists Are Crazy about Nuts." June 2017. Health.Harvard.edu/nutrition/why-nutritionists-are-crazy-about-nuts.

Intergovernmental Panel on Climate Change. *Special Report on Climate Change and Land*. Geneva, Switzerland, 2019.

Mayo Clinic. "How Plant-Based Food Helps Fight Cancer." October 30, 2019. MayoClinic.org/healthy-lifestyle/nutrition-and-healthy-eating/in-depth /how-plant-based-food-helps-fight-cancer/art-20457590.

Mayo Clinic. "The Power of a Plant-Based Diet for Heart Health." April 9, 2019. MayoClinic.org/power-plant-based-diet-for-heart-health/art-20454743.

Medline Plus, s.v. "Healthy Food Trends—Beans and Legumes." Accessed January 21, 2021, MedlinePlus.gov/ency/patientinstructions/000726.htm.

Physicians Committee for Responsible Medicine. "Weight Loss: Reach a Healthy Weight with a Plant Based Diet." Accessed January 19, 2021. PCRM.org /health-topics/weight-loss.

Qian, F., G. Liu, F. B. Hu, S. N. Bhupathiraju, and Q. Sun. "Association between Plant-Based Dietary Patterns and Risk of Type 2 Diabetes: A Systematic Review and Meta-Analysis." *JAMA Internal Medicine* 179, no. 10 (2019): 1335–44. DOI.org/10.1001/jamainternmed.2019.2195.

INDEX

ACKNOWLEDGMENTS

First, we'd like to thank our family and friends for their endless love and support, especially Marc, who gave the most brutally honest taste tests and was always willing to hunt down ingredients for us. Thanks to Kristin, Ryan, and Sean D. for being our biggest cheerleaders. And Seany G., thank you for keeping us laughing and telling us it's all going to be okay. Special thanks to Granny, Gramps, and YaYa for instilling a love of family and food in us and passing along the family traditions. Bowie and Lucy and all the furbabies in our lives, thank you for being so darn cute and making us want to be better humans for you. We love you all to the moon and back!

Thank you to the whole Callisto team for believing in us and giving us this incredible opportunity. We could not have completed this book without the guidance and expertise of the super-talented Van Van Cleave. Your constant encouragement and editing prowess made this such an enjoyable process.

And to our YouTube viewers, none of this would have been possible without you. Your support and friendship over the years have meant the world to us, and we are so grateful that you've stuck with us after all this time. Much love!

ABOUT THE AUTHORS

Janet Dockery and **Maddie Dockery** are a mother-daughter team and the creators of the YouTube channels *Vegan as Fork* and *Madrosed*. They have been making videos together since 2007 about some of their favorite things: reality TV and delicious vegan food. They love spending time with their family and rescue pups, hiking and biking in the beautiful Hudson Valley, and binge-watching TV.

Janet has been cooking for more than 50 years, and one of her greatest joys in life is to watch family and friends enjoy her vegan culinary creations. Her goal is to encourage others to try out plant-based eating and show how easy and accessible maintaining a vegan lifestyle can be. She's always on the lookout for new ingredients or cuisines to try.

Maddie graduated from Syracuse University with a bachelor's degree in broadcast journalism in 2013. Go Orange! She is passionate about putting an end to animal cruelty throughout the world and hopes to inspire people to be more compassionate toward animals. In her spare time, you can find her ballroom or tap dancing, playing the ukulele, crocheting, or playing *Dungeons and Dragons*.